Permanent Employee

The Pros, Cons and Secrets

Permanent Employee: The Pros, Cons and Secrets

First Edition (2016)
Second Edition (2018)

Copyright © 2016, Richard Renstone

Published by Arthur Black Publishing

Library of Congress Control Number: 2016961646

ISBN-10: 0-9979596-2-2

ISBN-13: 978-0-9979596-2-8

Permanent Employee:
The Pros, Cons and Secrets

Richard Renstone

Edited by

Dr. Rita Mukherjee and Renato Antolovich

Cover Design

Renato Antolovich

DEDICATIONS

I dedicate my book to my loving wife,
who is my soulmate that
I can never live without.
I have asked my wife on many occasions,
where she was when she
was three, because we could have got
married then.

CONTENTS

INTRODUCTION

If you bought this book you may be a student, new graduate, or a workforce newbie searching for some valuable information to prepare you before setting off on your career journey. Maybe you're a professional interested in some new information, or frustrated and upset about your career because it's not really working out the way you thought it would. There are all kinds of reasons why you might be searching for information on employment and being an employee, it's triggered by a situation or circumstance at work that makes you feel uncomfortable.

There are all kinds of work situations you may face throughout our career to do with uncertainty, dismal outlook, job instability, or your retirement. It could be that you haven't had a pay raise since you started working or maybe you are being mistreated or subjected to expectations that are impossible to reach. You could feel isolated from your colleagues or you have experienced massive lay-offs. It also may be that your work environment and morale have significantly shifted negative. May be there is career path but you've been bypassed leaving you stuck in the same position while others have advanced even though you trained them.

Permanent Employee: The Pros, Cons and Secrets, provides you with valuable information you need to help you with your work situation. Why? It is based on over three decades of insight with real life work stories that will make you laugh, angry or sad but most importantly reveal employee realities that exist and the real truth behind them.

Permanent Employee: Pros, Cons and Secrets explores employment basics as, benefits, pay, holidays, pension, salary, and career advancement; then dives into examining why people become permanent employees by breaking down their mindset. This book explores the advantages and disadvantages of being an employee to inform the reader of where they stand as being an employee. Finally, this book uncovers the hidden beliefs that many employees subconsciously carry, that are a controlling force in employee's lives by creating worry, false fears and anxiety, resulting self-defeating and restrictive behaviors.

Change is waiting for you and it is up to you to step up and take charge of your own destiny.

THE EMPLOYEE

The employee is labelled by many people, employment agencies and companies, as a permanent employee, fulltime employee or just plain employee. However, the fulltime employee label doesn't work for me, since fulltime employment can be carried out whether or not the person is an employee or a consultant.

On the other hand, calling an employee, a permanent employee suggests that the worker is long-term, has an employer-employee relationship of some kind, meaning the worker displays a degree of commitment, stability, loyalty, security, and subordination. Also, the employee will perform duties according to the work schedule set out by the employer. Therefore, the employee will work any regular and irregular work hours the employer has set, and, the priority in which the employee performs their duties or responsibilities. Moreover, an employee must follow all corporate policies, standards, practices and procedures which includes employee pay scheme and pay period.

Employees receive pay according to the employer's pay schedule and policies. So, the permanent employee is dependent on the employer determining and controlling the amount of pay, the frequency of pay and the method in which the employee is paid. This means, the permanent employee is paid a wage for their service, usually a salary, which can be paid monthly, weekly, or bi-weekly usually on the 15th and 30th of the month, every second Friday or can even be a monthly payment. The rate of pay is usually calculated by using how many working days there are per year.

Most importantly, a permanent employee receives a NET paycheck, which is derived after many deductions are subtracted from the GROSS paycheck amount. The paycheck deductions all correspond to the employee's benefits package and government deduction requirements.

Initially, employee benefit package and government deductions include, but are not limited to, such items as:

- Medical

- Dental

- Accidental death

- Life insurance

- Long and short term disability

- Vision care

- Prescription drugs

- Psychologist sessions

- Massage therapy

- Physiotherapy

- Employee assistance services

- Paid holidays

- Paid floater days

- Paid sick days

- Federal taxes

- Provincial or state taxes

- Employment or unemployment insurance

- Pension plan coverage either company or government based or both, and

- Maternity leave

Medical costs and coverage vary because of government funding and other supplementary supports. Keep in mind that dental, medical and prescription drugs and other coverage will have variations based on age group, country, state, or province. For instance, in the United Kingdom medical coverage is free for all UK citizens. Dental coverage is free but only for certain individuals. To view additional dental coverage restrictions in the UK visit the following URL:

http://www.nhs.uk/chq/Pages/1786.aspx?CategoryID=74

Furthermore, in the United Kingdom, a permanent employee must seek and secure their own insurance for dental and prescription drug coverage since they are not free. However, there are exceptions. Prescription drugs are only free for any child up to 16 years of age and for seniors 60 years old and over.

Generally all benefit plan costs are deducted from an employee's paycheck with a few exceptions. For instance, if an employee had to purchase a benefits package from an insurance company as an individual, the cost would be substantially higher or even more than double. The reason is the benefit package an employee pays for is only a portion of the full cost, because the employer usually pays 50% or more of the total cost. However, when it comes to government related deductions, such as, pension plans and employment insurance, the employer pays at least double the costs even though this is obscure to the employee.

Some employee's benefits packages may also include, a company pension plan, or another type of retirement savings plan like, in Canada, a Registered Retirement Savings Plan (RRSP) or in the U.S. a 401K or in the United Kingdom, a private pension plan.

Any government based deductions are more geared towards state, provincial or federal taxes, government benefits or programs which include some items like, retirement pension, employment or unemployment insurance or national insurance and so on. The percentages for each deduction vary because they are calculated according to country of residence, marital status and the income amount. Employees must pay for all benefits package and government deductions because all of them are mandatory and to many employees the cost may seem high.

Keep in mind that many people are confused when looking at their paycheck and many just assume it is all tax and then wonder why taxes are so high. The reason is total deductions from an employee's GROSS paycheck will range from 28% to 50%. Note that these deductions include benefits package and government deductions so it's not only tax. For example, in the US, federal tax is at a rate of 11%, state tax is 4%, and social security is 6.2%. In Canada, federal tax is 10%, provincial is 7%, pension is 5% and employment insurance is 2%. Note that deduction percentages are all based on the employee's location, the amount of income, and marital status.

Therefore if the employee lives in Nevada or in South Carolina and so on, is married or not, will make a difference but also the higher the income the higher the deductions. Deductions are a part of what a permanent employee must pay for being an employee with benefits.

To find out more information about actual tax rates go to the following websites:

For Canada:

http://www.cra-arc.gc.ca/tx/ndvdls/fq/txrts-eng.html

For the United States of America:

http://www.irs.com/articles/2014-federal-tax-rates-personal-exemptions-and-standard-deductions

For the United Kingdom:

https://www.gov.uk/income-tax-rates/current-rates-and-allowances

So far we have reviewed some of the basics of being a permanent employee, by examining the work relationship, pay, and deductions, but that's not enough, since there are more gaps to uncover. Another main gap to explore is the employee mindset, which is actually what determines why people choose to be a permanent employee in the first place.

EMPLOYEE MINDSET

The employee mindset is a combination of many things that together, make a person become an employee. What I have found is employees generally stay long-term, for 20 to 30 years or more, which is a generational aspect that my parents retained, as well as, some of my generation.

This mindset was to get a job, work hard and stay with the same company until retirement, without the need for advancement and higher wages but just to be grateful for making a living and having a good job. These attitudes were based on fear and usually coming from an immigrant standpoint like my father and mother had. In the end, the permanent employee would finally retire only to find themselves in the grave a few years later.

So, is staying at the same job a disadvantage for people? The answer is, yes and no. I say this since it depends on the individual. Some people are happy to sit in the same job day after day and go with the flow which is generally union type jobs. On the other hand, others working in non-union type employment want to improve their lives and hop around in search of more opportunities with better environments, higher pay, and better benefits and so on.

However, workers who stay for their entire work life in non-union environments may at some point risk being phased out by technologies, or reach a point where they can't get a job elsewhere because they have allowed themselves to stagnate and lack the required skill sets. If employees continue to gain the required skills as they putter along in the same job, they generally are not at risk of being tossed a side but end up staying with the company.

Overall the main theme of employees is, they are individuals that require consistency, safety and security with very little drama and instability in their lives when it comes to their income, job security and especially retirement. This rational sets up employees to be loyal, making them cling to a long term employee type situation.

This employee mindset is generally based on feelings of insecurity, which is created by having current and future fears mainly about failure. Some of the negative biased thoughts or dialogue of the employee's mindset is based on negative or inaccurate thoughts something like:

- I don't want to lose my job, because I will have to start selling everything

- If I lose my job, I will lose my car, house, and everything else I have

- If I lose my job, I will lose my pension, maybe my spouse will leave me

- I can't cope with job expectations and stress, high output, efficiency and productivity

- I will be replaced when I get older then what do I do?

- I'll get fired because I do poorly at every job I do

- I'm stupid and can't get anything right...

- I was fired before and I don't want that to happen again

- I don't know where I can get another job like this one

- Got to pay my bills

- The company will take care of me

- I have company benefits, medical, dental, accidental death...that I need

- I can't lose my paid holidays, floater and sick days

- I belong to a union, I am protected, and guaranteed

- I am guaranteed 40 hours a week and a paycheck

- They can't replace me I've got a lot of experience here

- What will I do when I am retired, will I have money to retire?

- What happens if I die?

- Who will take care of me if I become sick or very ill and can't work?

- With all the economic downturns and instability at least I have a job

- The company is strong and will protect me from economic turmoil

- I have enough seniority now they can never get rid of me...

- I am committed to working for this company so they will do the same

- I don't want to have stress in my life; I just want to work until I retire

- I will get replaced by someone younger when I get older and lose my job

So, most of the employee's thoughts and beliefs are based on a negative future and are coming from within the individual. The employee achieves this by their thoughts predicting or projecting a negative future or outcome about their job, pay, income, old age, and retirement to name a few.

This thought process in psychological circles refers to anticipatory thoughts which in general terms signify the person anticipates a negative outcome in the future related to failure at their job, which could result in being fired, divorced, loss of their home, possessions, or no money at retirement or having no pension, and/or even getting some incapacitating illness, and so on.

These kinds of thoughts, consequently, create the worries, fear and anxiety the employees feel. The reality is these thoughts are generated within regardless of the person having no real concrete, or tangible evidence to have or support such thoughts. In essence, the employees are predictors of a negative future for themselves because they may have low, self-esteem, self-confidence and self-worth. These kinds of qualities are the basic building blocks for this kind of negatively biased mindset. Where does this employee bias and negativity start?

First of all, this employee mindset and choosing to become an employee usually starts at a very early age. Since, believe it or not, we all learn to play, "worker, employee or even business person" from our parent or parents. With that in mind, many permanent employee types are no different from their permanent employee parents. I say this because we all watch, listen and through osmosis, learn from our parents about defining what a job is, what working is, what a paycheck is, what hours to work, and how to make money. We also learn and see firsthand, all the associated feelings of frustration, anxiety, worry and anguish involved with employment, and money. We also record, the hardships and the attitudes our parents had about work and most importantly their fears.

As children we learn by listening to all the conversations and comments our parents make and discuss during breakfast, or at the supper table, or while watching television in the living room, or while speaking to their friends on the phone and so on. We also watch our parent or parent's work routines. For instance, we see them getting ready in the morning; having breakfast and coffee; packing their lunches and ours, setting off to go to work; to drop us off and pick us up from school or daycare; or if they bring work home with them, or have to stay late and on and on. This happens regardless, if our parents are teachers, lawyers, scientists, social workers, professors, programmers, engineers, plumbers, doctors, welders or whatever their profession is. Our parents also provide us with career and work information by speaking to us directly.

Practically all parents provide guidance, words of advice and wisdom to their child or children so they too will do the right thing in regard to employment and careers. Likewise, our parents may have a government job such as, a professor at a university or college, or work in a government office, or may have a union based job. From this, we are told or through osmosis to get a similar government based or union job just like our parents have.

After this kind of exposure and learning experience voila we, become a permanent employee because it's the right thing to do since, this is what kind of job our parents had. In other words, many of us have a similar job or career as our parents because through their influence and teachings, we inherit their mindset, opinions, insecurities, fears and anxiety about life and especially the workplace.

For instance, when I was growing up, my father was a plumber and of course always under stress and worrying about finances. A couple of my brothers wanted to be a plumber like my father, while another brother wanted to be a firefighter, and I wanted to be a medical doctor to help people.

Even with all of these childhood hopes and dreams we had, I remember my father specifically telling us to never be a plumber because it was a dirty and unhealthy job, even though at the time and even today it is a very lucrative trade to be in. Instead, we became engineers, managers, and consultants, but first we all became permanent employees just like our parents.

Dealing with the Fears

After working as a permanent employee at many companies I observed and found some of the factors involved that helped many employees alleviate their fears, worries and anxiety and it started with becoming a permanent employee.

First of all employees are, "permanent". If we look at the dictionary meaning of "permanent" it states, "a long lasting or intended to last or remain unchanged indefinitely". Interestingly enough, just the word "permanent" itself, projects commitment which is fulfilled and supported by the employee-employer relationship that exists.

This relationship can be compared to any intimate relationships we are familiar with such as, friendships, marriages, and so on which also establish the sense of safety, trust, and security. A permanent employee position also paves the path to feeling that nothing will change and therefore having no need to worry which in fact keeps all fears and anxiety at reasonable levels.

Can you recall the first time you were showing up to a new job, like how nervous, scared and anxious you were? Having sweaty palms, and maybe even some stomach or digestive problems, because everything was new and you didn't know anyone. After being at the job for a month or so, all of it gradually disappears. The reason, you start to relax and become familiar with co-workers, your job, and have developed routines. More importantly you surpassed that nail biting three month probationary period.

Employees also use repetition and familiarity to ease their workplace anxiety, tension and fears. Employees accomplish this by staying at a job for many years to attain a senior level of experience where they learn all aspects of it. They perform the same tasks and decisions day after day and during that period form long-term relationships with co-workers. All people, including myself like to feel comfortable, with very little worry or doubt, in fact we all seem to thrive for familiarity, at the workplace and at home. Most of us also need to establish routines in all areas of life, both personal and professional, since it provides a means of familiarity, consistency and stability.

For instance, a routine at work may be, as soon as you get there, you see Rita in the elevator and you both have a short chat about the game last night. Then you get off the elevator proceed down the hall toward your desk or office, then, you look into Ted's office to see him at his desk, and say good morning. You arrive at your office, take your jacket off, turn on the computer, get up and go to the coffee room with "your" personal coffee cup to get a coffee…

As employees, there are no sudden surprises or confusion, since we have already surpassed those. We all know the coffee machine location and who Bill is, what Julie does and that both of them are on the third floor and why Judy talks like that to everyone or that Hank is always grumpy… All of these things are familiar and routine, making employees feel comfortable in their surroundings and workplace settings.

This familiarity and feeling comfortable reminds me of a short story about how I made a new hire feel comfortable. I remember working for a field service company and I was a senior employee and was a smoker at the time. All the smokers would smoke at this table that was set out in the back shop area away from all the offices.

At this workplace, many of the employees would play soccer during the lunch period as long as there were enough people to form two teams. I can recall on a Tuesday, anyone that was available went out to play a game of soccer. However during this lunchtime game it was different. One of the players, Richard, was running fiercely after the ball to find out when he looked up, he slammed his face into a fence post. This poor fellow broke his nose, had two black eyes and drove his front bottom teeth through the skin between his lower lip and chin which required over 25 stitches. Richard was an easy going person, a happy-go-lucky sort of attitude but this situation was very unfortunate.

Later that afternoon, when he returned from the hospital, you could see his whole face was swollen, black, blue and red, absolutely awful and looked very painful. He had some difficulty in speaking since his bottom lip and face was so swollen but you could still understand him. Nonetheless, he was in good spirits knowing that it would all eventually heal.

The following day, I arrived at work and had a cup of coffee in hand and was standing at the smoking table having a cigarette. All of the sudden a horn sounded telling me that someone was at the front door wanting to get in. I put my coffee down and immediately walked over to see it was a new hire, Phil. The operations manager told us about Phil the day before.

So, I opened the door and shook his hand and said, "Good morning Phil, I'm Rick, welcome aboard, can I get you a cup of coffee or something?" He looked shy and nervous and said, "Well...ah...sure that would be great, um... is there any place... where I can put my lunch and then have a smoke?" We went into the coffee room and he placed his lunch in the fridge, grabbed a cup of coffee and we went into the back shop to the smoking table.

We were standing at the smoking table drinking coffee and talking about what it is like to work at this company, then discussed the training he would receive and all the documentation that he could review that day, just to get him feeling comfortable and bring him up to speed. I could empathize with being at work the first day on the job, all nervous and unsure not knowing anyone or what lies ahead or if you'll fit in and so on... We continued with smoking and talking and he was feeling quite relaxed.

So here I was making this new hire, Phil feel comfortable and relaxed then I heard the back door slam. I didn't know who it was because many people used the back door to get to their office. The person who arrived turned out to be Richard, and he was walking toward us.

As Richard approached us, we could see how gruesome and beat up he looked, with his face swollen, black and blue with stitches. At that moment, I looked right at Richard pointing and shaking my finger at him, I said, "And the next time you son-of-a-bitch it's gonna be a lot worse!" Of course, Richard being the happy go lucky guy he was, joined into the act and started shaking as if he was scared and then briskly ran through the doorway.

I looked at Phil, he had no pigment in his face, white with fright, scared out of his mind, he was shaking, avoiding eye contact, and confused. I am sure he was wondering how this psychopath could beat this person to a pulp and still be employed.

Anyway, I looked at Phil again and said, "Relaaax" and started laughing. I immediately started telling him the truth behind what happened to Richard and his soccer accident. Phil let out a big sigh of relief, and calmed down and started to laugh. He said, "Wow, I was really scared of you after seeing what Richard looked like." I replied, "Hey no worries shit like that doesn't happen here I was just trying to get a laugh".

Other personal routines we have to make us feel comfortable may be after work like; going to pick up your kids from daycare or your parents' house, and while driving home you talk to your kids about their day. Then you arrive home, your kids run into the house ahead of you; you get in the door, make a cup of tea or coffee or have a beer, sit down turn on the television, or read the newspaper.

You relax, for about a half hour or so, then you get up and start making supper, and your spouse shows up and so on. Of course, we all have important routines that we need in order to feel comfortable. There are other things that make us feel comfortable especially like being a permanent employee with a benefits package.

The employee benefits package calms many fears and reassures that they are covered and taken care of, in case of any unexpected medical, dental, accidental death, or serious illness that leaves an employee unable to work, or to have huge unaffordable medical bills. The employee benefits packages support the employee which in turn makes them feel safe and secure.

Another form of calming fears is employees are also locked into a regular paycheck with paid holidays, and sick days. The employees always know they will be paid every two weeks without any worries about losing the regular pay which again reinforces the feelings of commitment and security. In fact when it comes to a paycheck the employee can almost set their watch to the time they receive their pay.

Another reassurance the permanent employee has is that they have a connection that they are a part of a group, a family and department. Additionally, the permanent employee is also accepted, acknowledged for their voice, opinion, experience and knowledge. This again, ensures the employee that they are valued and worthy of the position they hold which helps their self-esteem and self-worth.

Lastly employees have a pension plan for their retirement. Retirement for many is a thought process of being taken care of in their later years with no financial or medical upheavals. An employee's pension alleviates the fear they have about their future retirement.

All of these points we have discussed so far add up to taking care of the employee's needs so they feel safe, secure, have the ability to forecast into a stable future, to know that there will always be another pay check and in the end a pension. These were some of the norms I had in my mind at one point that made me feel stable, secure, reduced the worries about life, finances and my future.

After discussing the general mindset that drives employees, we still have to fill a huge gap with regards to the advantages and disadvantages are when being a permanent employee. I found that these are what make employees, employees.

THE PROS AND CONS

After all the experiences I have had as an employee, I found there were many advantages to it but also many disadvantages. In this section, I will discuss contrasts that exist when being an employee. Keep in mind that we all have different upbringings, focus, values and morality which all play a role in forming our outlook on life and work. Some of you may feel that being an employee has no disadvantages, or that there may be a few to add to the ones I discuss.

Your views and experiences may be different from what I point out because being an employee may work for you entirely. I believe that people in general have to do whatever works for them. However, with any role, there are advantages and disadvantages, and most importantly if the disadvantages outweigh the advantages, we tend to look for another option, like an alternative role or job or look for something completely different.

So, first let's explore some of the advantages we all have as permanent employees.

Page Left Blank

EMPLOYEE ADVANTAGES

In this section I discuss some of the employee advantages that I have found and experienced while being a permanent employee. All of these advantages may vary depending on the country, state or province you live in, as well as, working for a particular company or corporation. Even though geographic location somewhat influences these advantages I have listed, they are still applicable and are very similar in nature because the human factor plays a significant role.

REGULAR PAY

One advantage I found when working as an employee was receiving a regular paycheck like clockwork. This was money, a source of income I would receive usually every two weeks or bi-weekly, like on the 15th and the 30th of every month or every 2nd Friday. Sometimes, depending on the company, some employees can even be paid weekly but that is quite rare and I didn't personally ever experience it.

The consistency in paychecks to me, was fantastic, a regular paycheck to keep me from worrying about money, bills and other related stuff. This is one of the elements that provided consistency and foresight for me as an employee and fulfilled one of my needs that I could always count on.

DENTAL COVERAGE

Dental coverage is a part of an employee's benefits package and is helpful, except that there are some limitations and restrictions on coverage. Nonetheless, I found that the cost for crowns and other dental appliances are covered up to 50%. This is still an exceptional deal since employees are getting a discount on basic dental work and each six month cleaning and check-up that provides the employee with incentive to ensure they have excellent dental health. At one point, I found the larger the company you work for the better dental coverage you would have, however now all dental coverage is very similar.

EXTENDED MEDICAL COVERAGE

Extended medical coverage is also a part of the employee benefits package and includes, ninety percent coverage on prescription drugs and a certain coverage amount for other items such as, psychology sessions, massage and physio therapy, and so on. The medical coverage one receives does differ based on geographic location, the insurance company and their actual employer.

For instance, in the US, the company you work for will usually provide you with a medical plan but keep in mind you may have to purchase additional coverage.

If you live in the United Kingdom, almost all medical is covered by the government and is free, but items like prescription drugs and dental work are not covered. Therefore an employee in the UK will have to find separate prescription drug and dental coverage.

In Canada, employees rely on the medical coverage supplied by the employer, but also must pay for provincial medical coverage that is mandatory. Payments for this coverage vary in each province. For example, in Alberta there is no charge, while Ontario residents must pay via direct paycheck deductions or by using other financial channels.

Overall this coverage is still positive, regardless if paying for it or not, because as we all know, we need it.

LIFE, ACCIDENTAL DEATH AND DISMEMBERMENT

This is another employee benefit, which is intended to protect them and their family in the event of accidental death or dismemberment. The coverage depends on location of course but also is based on salary, which is used to calculate what payout amount would be granted in case of sudden or accidental death. Usually the awarded amount is two times the employee's salary if the employee dies or has total paralysis. This payout is a bonus either way you look at it since, this could help your loved ones to carry on, as well as, cover funeral costs, personal debt and other associated costs without worry.

PENSION PLAN

A pension plan in my opinion is the most important part of being an employee. Pension plan benefits are also one of the main reasons why people are employed with a company for life. The pension plan in fact equates to, the employee being taken care of in their later years. This I feel is one of the top advantages of being an employee if you get the right company and pension plan.

So, which pension is the right one? Pension plans have a couple of different schemes. The first one is when the employer matches the employee's contribution up to a certain yearly limit. Employee contributions are regularly deducted from the employee's paycheck. The other pension scheme involves the company having its own pension plan which still requires employee contributions that are deducted from the employee's paycheck. However, this scheme pays the employee a specific amount at retirement. These two pension schemes are the most popular types and are called defined contribution pension and defined benefit pension respectively.

In my opinion, a defined benefit program is the best one to choose because this plan has a set income amount the employee will receive after 20, 30, or 40 years of service.

In this situation the employer has made a commitment to take care of its employee through setting aside a sum of money, a pension fund that is used for employee pensions. The employee has no worries or doesn't have to make any decisions just stay with the company for the minimum amount of time required in order to receive their pension. The amount of pension employees receive is based on factors like tenure at the company, number of years contributed to the pension plan and what their average salary was in the last 5 years of employment. However, I have seen this pension scheme fade away quickly from the pension world.

The defined contribution pension is becoming more common because it's up to the employee to make decisions based on what shares, mutual funds and other investment instruments they will use to invest for their own future, and pension fund. In this schema, employees contribute and then the company contributes matching a percentage of the employee's contribution to a maximum yearly amount.

Any of these pension schemes are a decent plan regardless if they are defined benefit or contribution. In addition, any of these pension plans are especially beneficial for those individuals who have problems saving money for their future retirement.

STOCK OPTIONS

I have worked for a few companies that offered stock options. Options are generally a good deal anywhere you work, at least most of the time. Stock options are mainly used to,

- Offer employees additional financial compensation

- Retain and attract employees

- Provide a profitable incentive for those employees who purchase Call Stock Options

- To help the company's stock price rise

- Make employees feel like owners or partners in the company they work for and

- Provide confidence to the employee about the company and its future

Employee stock options are comparable to stock exchange traded call options but issued by the employer. In simple terms a call option means that the person who buys them believes the stock price will rise. In the past, options were offered to executive management. Now more and more companies offer stock options to all of their employee's as a part of the employee benefits package and as a form of supplementary compensation.

The employee can buy options by deductions off their paycheck, or can purchase them outright. When the employee purchases stock options, they have the right to purchase a set of company stocks after a certain timeframe or vesting period, and at a set price or strike price which is all determined by the employer. The set price of the option is called the strike price and is ordinarily set at the current market price or a higher price than the current market price of the stocks (shares). The vesting period for the options is usually set at a future date. In order for the employee to exercise the option or convert the options into shares two conditions must be met. First the vesting period date must be expired and second, the current stock price must be higher than the strike price.

For example, an employee decides to purchase 100 stock options which allow the employee the right but not obligation to purchase 100 company shares. The company has set the strike price to $10 per share, with a vesting period of one year. The employee will pay for the options by paycheck deductions. This means the employee allows the company to deduct the amount of the cost of 100 shares at $10 each for a total of $1000 from their paycheck. These payments from their paycheck are in increments of $200 bi-weekly. After five weeks the employee owns the options. This gives the employee the option to buy 100 shares of the company stock at a strike price of $10 per share. The vesting period set on the option to buy the shares at $10 per share is one year from the date the employee received the options.

At this point, the current stock price is $8 per share so the employee cannot exercise their options because the two conditions have not been met. During the one year vesting period the employee has been monitoring the stock price and has seen it rise to $25 per share and now the one year vesting period is expired. At this time, the employee exercises their options meaning the employee converts the options into shares and is free to sell or do what they wish with the shares. In this case, the employee decides to sell 100 shares at $25 a share for a profit of $15 per share or $1,500 profit minus any commissions. Keep in mind that there are many variations on company stock options and any profit or capital gains on the shares are taxed according to government regulations and laws.

Regardless of commissions and taxes stock options in my opinion are an excellent bonus and are a good balance for added employee compensation. When dealing with stock options I have never lost money myself nor have seen anyone else lose money.

However make an important note when dealing with stock options:

(1) Keep in mind that with any market trading there is always risk of losses

(2) If by chance the employee lost their job or got fired during the vesting period, they lose the stock options since the contract is usually void.

PAID HOLIDAYS

Holidays…finally…let's pack up and go! Paid holidays are the norm for any permanent employee.

Generally the employee is restricted to a minimum of two weeks of paid holidays in the beginning of their employment; however some companies start their new employees at three weeks. Make note that a week of holidays is really five working days off not seven.

As an employee continues to work year after year, they continue to accumulate and increase holiday length at certain yearly milestones. For example, an employee after five years of service increments their holidays from two weeks to three weeks and after 10 years of service from three weeks to four weeks. After 20 years of service the employee is given another week to bring it to a total of five weeks holidays. The positive spin on holidays is the employee is paid full wages for each day of their holidays, so there is no interruption of income.

I can recall at one point employees could stack their holidays year after year. Some coworkers would never take holidays for periods up to 20 years, thus accumulating a large amount of holidays. Unfortunately today employers have caught on to this and have stopped or restricted this practice, generally making employees take their holidays each year. Keep in mind that each company is different and has its own policies that govern employee holidays.

PAID SICK DAYS

In addition to paid holidays, employees have another advantage which is paid sick days. Usually companies provide an employee with 10 to 12 sick days per year but of course this will differ from company to company. Sick days are working days used anytime an employee is ill and must stay home. When the employee is at home sick they are paid full wages for each sick day thus having no pay disruptions or loss of pay.

Companies at one point would allow employees to stack their sick days if they were not used. However, I have found that companies are phasing out this policy, since numerous employees would stack sick days for decades because they never get sick or sick enough to stay home. They would then use these stacked sick days and stacked holidays to take early retirement at full wage for a few months before their pension commences.

Now most companies have changed their policy so employees will lose their sick days if they are not used during the year. However, some companies allow employees to carry over some of their sick days to the following year but that's as far as they go, otherwise if they are not used they are lost.

I recall a little story about when I was working for a government based entity and all the employees had a very similar mindset about sick days. I remember taking a couple of sick days because I was ill with a bad cold. When I returned to work, a few coworkers approached me and asked, "Where were you these past couple days?" I said, "Well I was sick I had a bad cold so I took couple of sick days" they replied "What! What are you doing?

Why waste a paid day off when you can use those days for mental health days to get away from here and enjoy yourself instead."

PAID FLOATER DAYS

Paid floater days are an advantage and a part of the employee benefits package. Each year the employee has a set number of paid floater or personal days which is usually 10 to 12 days per year but the amount will vary since they are set by company policy. So floater days allow the employee to avoid having a loss of income or pay disruptions. These floater days can be used at the employee's discretion but generally people use them for personal incidentals.

Incidentals most times require the employee to attend or to be somewhere during regular working hours, such as, car repair, a child's graduation, weddings, cable installation, furnace repair or maintenance, day surgery and so on.

These were also stackable just like the sick days and holidays, but many companies again are steering away from this practice too. Consequently, employees must use the floaters days before year-end otherwise they lose them.

PAID TRAINING

Training for each employee is paid for by the company or the employee pays out of pocket then to be reimbursed. During training the employee is paid their regular wage and do not lose any pay. In addition, the company will pay for all training expenses and associated costs which cover items such as, training materials, travel, accommodations, flights, meals, car rentals and other items.

The company will provide and pay for training courses that are internal, external or third party. Any of the courses can be in classroom, or online such as, eLearning, pre-recorded or live webinar. Additionally, the company will purchase, training material such as books, videos, DVDs, and audio recordings. Training material supported by the company pertains to topics specific to the company and its employees. Some training topics may be, ISO 9001, ITIL, project management, risk management, change management, company policies, cost engineering, various certifications, quality assurance, self-improvement, ethics and software courses and so on.

Training is a bonus for any employee because many training courses are usually very expensive and provide the employee with the opportunity of adding new skill sets or updating current ones that can immediately be used on the job thus making employees a valuable asset.

JOB SECURITY

The definition of "job security" is set by each individual since it's whatever it means to the individual. I say this because most people have their own interpretation and definition of what it means. Generally, employees feel that security means their employer provides lifelong employment so they will not lose their job, and have a steady paycheck. This also includes having regular salary increases usually 2% to 3% that are based on merit or cost of living or both. Security also involves a pension plan and other benefits that cover medical, dental, paid holidays, sick days, floater days , etc. and all of this is a wonderful recipe for having a sense of security.

Having security keeps employees comfortable with their work life, pay and feel life is easier. The majority of permanent employees are usually searching for secure jobs within large companies, or government entities that are unionized. The reason is once employed by these large companies, especially union based jobs; they can effortlessly acquire any kind of credit. Some of the credit vehicles include such items as, mortgages, lines of credit, credit cards or any other credit instruments they wish to have.

Additionally, this advantage allows employees to enjoy security, since it helps them from worrying about their future, losing their job or income and know they will always be employed until they retire, which could be as long as 20 to 40 years or a lifetime.

UNION

I have worked a couple of union based jobs and I recall one was for a government agency. I found that working there was okay, the people and environment was acceptable too. What I found was this type of job was mainly for individuals that only want to work for a company, have a position and were not driven or looking for career advancement. By this I am referring to those individuals who need security, a steady income, benefits, and the support and strength of a union. Moreover, they don't mind just doing the same job day in day out, because it supports the employee feeling secure about their job and livelihood.

When I was at this job, working in maintenance, I found it was merely impossible to get fired, since I saw people, stealing packages and boxes, package contents, credit cards, and some even making death threats. What would happen to these individuals? The union would intervene; the employee would be given a short suspension with or without pay and then be reinstated shortly after.

This practice only reinforces the employee's sense of security since it is like being untouchable, and don't lose their job, regardless of the circumstances. This of course I have never agreed with, since there must be limits and consequences for employee's actions. Consequently, as unionized employees we were able to do almost anything without problems or the threat of losing our jobs.

For instance, I was on night shift based on having the lowest union seniority level. Regardless, I tried making the best of it and having fun like I do at any other job I have had. I recall working the night shift in the plant and we were ahead of schedule with our tasks. A co-worker, Lester and I, started to make up an entertainment plan. As a joke, we wanted to leave something for the day shift that started at 7 am. While we were in the back area of the maintenance shop, I lay down on the floor with my left arm bent at 90 degrees from the elbow facing up and my right arm bent, at 90 degrees facing downward. My legs were positioned with my left leg straight and the right leg bent at 90 degrees with my heel almost touching my butt. As soon as I was in position, Lester proceeded to outline my body on the floor with masking tape just as they do on the murder-mystery crime shows you see on TV.

While Lester was outlining, another coworker from a different department was walking by and stopped. They asked if the person on the floor was okay and I immediately lifted my head, laughed and stated that it was all good. Then the coworker came over to see what we were up to; as they got closer you could hear laughter get louder and louder. We completed our masking tape masterpiece and were proud of our accomplishment. Finally our shift came to an end and the day shift started. Many on the day shift were amused by this gift we had left on the floor. On top of it all we received many compliments for our creative work.

Another thing to add is that it was against the law for any employee to be drug tested because it was against their rights. Is that security or what? You can be an employee with numerous substance abuse problems, be under the influence and keep getting paid without any consequences. Of course, there are always exceptions to the rule, such as being employed as an aviation or health care professional and so on which brings up another example.

CAREER ADVANCEMENT

First career advancement depends on the company and the structure it has in place. So in this section I will only focus on discussing non-union type companies because unions have a seniority structure. In an ideal world, employees generally can move up the career ladder, because of their performance, quality of work, productivity, professionalism, interpersonal skills, education, training, and years of experience.

Career advancement can happen rapidly in a public or private sector, within non-unionized companies, because there are usually new opportunities being created due to rapid rate of expansion and growth, employee movement and turnover, and having a progressive structure in place. Public and private sector companies in most cases are open to providing solid pathways for employees so they can advance their career, attain higher status and gain higher pay.

For instance, while I was working for a public traded field service company, I was able to catapult my career from a trainee to a junior level within seven months, surpassing the average period of 12 to 18 months. Then continued to advance to an international technical advisor position within 2 ½ years. This advancement was phenomenal and proof of a career pathway, since international employment was usually offered to senior employees with a minimum of 7 to 10 years of experience.

The other side of career advancement is all up to the individual. Some people want to advance into new or different positions while others are happy just doing the same job with slow movement if any. Advancement in a career is based on how determined, ambitious, and driven the person is, as well as, their interpersonal skills, expectations, needs and most importantly their values.

Career advancement is a huge benefit for all employees as long as it is exactly what they are looking for, as it advances people into different career positions and salary increases, elevating a person's livelihood and lifestyle.

NO LIABILITY

When employees are working at the office, in the shop, or out in a field location, there is always some kind of risk or liability. However, an employee generally has no worries about additional expenses for liability or attaining coverage because the employee is fully covered for any liabilities by their employer. General third party liability insurance covers such items as,

- Injuries to customers, employees, vendors or visitors that occur at the company workplace

- Injuries that have occurred outside the company's workplace that resulted because of an employee's actions from negligence

- Third party property damage caused by the company's employee

Some employers are insured through an insurance company while very large companies can be self-insured.

LONG TERM FORECASTING

Long term forecasting is usually made by corporations and companies in respect to their financial outlook and business strategies. However, as far as permanent employees are concerned, they have steady and verified income, especially when they are working for a large company, government entity and/or unionized employer. A permanent employee has an advantage to forecast long-term income since the income is the same for each bi-weekly or monthly pay period for years into the future.

With this in mind, it is quite normal for employees to plan for long term goals and purchases, since their income and job is considered by banking institutions to be very stable. However, banks require that an employee has worked at the same company for at least 6 months to 2 years. As long as they qualify, banks are generally wide open to provide credit proportional to the employee's income level.

With long term forecasting in mind, employees in unionized or government based jobs tend to take on long-term debt to make large purchases such as homes, fifth wheels, campers, jet skis, motorcycles, and other toys they feel are necessary. These union and/or government employees fit right into the "buy now pay later" scheme of things that is offered everywhere.

CORE AND KEY PERSONNEL

Core personnel are the individuals that make up a large group within a company that are considered as the foundation of the company's employee base. These individuals all play minor and major roles within the company and are permanent employees who continue to work with no thoughts of ever moving or leaving the company.

There is another elite group referred to as key personnel and only certain employees are considered as key personnel. This elite group makes up a vital body, making important and critical departmental, group or company decisions that affect the department, division or company as a whole, both administratively and financially. This

43

means that this group is responsible for the company's future actions going forward.

People that are usually selected for this key group are senior individuals who are keeners, with high productivity, genuinely committed, with excellent job performance and interpersonal skills. The employees are highly motivated, knowledgeable, experienced and are team players. Usually the key personnel group includes people who are CEOs, VPs, directors, senior management, and senior personnel. Now how is that for status?

I recall working for an inspection company, when I was chosen to be the lead person trained on the highest technological and most current instrument the company had designed. I was trained in the field by the senior electronics engineer and the senior scientist. We would perform services with the instrument and would encounter instrument design problems. As a group we would come up with solutions and ideas to iron out the design flaws and problems.

After this training and testing period, a support crew and I conducted services with this instrument around the world. I spent a few years breaking the international market with this instrument and produced all the training and support documentation. After that I became a part of the elite key personnel group. This group consisted of the CEO, manager of operations, head of research and development, lead design engineers, senior scientists as well as, myself and a few other senior level field staff. We were making decisions that controlled the company's future, such as policy, standards, procedures, strategic brainstorming, training requirements, human resources issues and other decisions.

When I reached this level of recognition, it made me feel important and special, that I was actually chosen as one of the top employees to make company decisions on policy that would affect the company's future. In fact, it was motivating and overwhelming. It made me want to work for the company even more and to do a better job than I was already doing.

Page Left Blank

EMPLOYEE DISADVANTAGES

After reviewing and discussing all those advantages, I am sure you are ready to explore the disadvantages. These disadvantages I have found are many and hopefully will not be a shocker. In essence what works for each person is up to the individual. I say this because some of you may feel there may be none at all, or disagree with some I have listed or if there is any, they may be so puny that it's a waste of time. In this section, I will discuss some of the things I found were disadvantages when I was a permanent employee.

YOUR HOURS

As an employee you are obligated to work at minimum within a range of 37 to 44 hours per week. The company requires employees to work this range of hours because most employees pay is calculated on a yearly basis, including all working days and statutory holidays. This information is then broken down into monthly, bi-weekly and hourly pay. Therefore, missing a couple hours of work is unacceptable as far as the accounting department is concerned, because each employee is paid according to the calculated yearly formula.

So, if these mandatory set hours are broken up by the employee taking a few hours off, it is generally frowned upon since it alters the calculated salary resulting in the employee owing the company hours. In this situation, the employee is tracked by administrative staff to ensure the employee makes up the few hours that were lost. This tracking and chasing done by an administrative support person in my experience generally is comparable to a parent chasing a child about the hours they owe.

The employee must work extra hours to make up for the hours they owe; however, these makeup hours are not regular hours but considered overtime as they are outside of normal working hours. Overtime hours and are usually paid at time and a half or double time, but not in this case. In fact, the employee takes regular time off only to give the company back overtime hours. How does that work? It doesn't benefit the employee because it's almost like a penalty for taking time off.

Another lost hour scenario to add to this is the employee may be forced to take a floater day in lieu to cover the lost time. Is this type of scenario fair? In my humble opinion, trading a whole day for a few hours isn't fair at all.

To me it seems like a sure disadvantage and frustrating, being chased around by the admin and forced to work overtime hours in lieu of or to take a full floater day off when only a couple hours are at stake.

LOW PAY

As an employee, companies pay lower wages based on the remuneration which includes combining a wage, plus the full benefits package which represents the employee's entire compensation package. Each company has their own cost calculation for how much the benefit packages cost per year. However, according to the U.S. Department of Labor the employees benefit package alone can account for up to 30 percent of the total remuneration.

For instance, if the employee is single and has a paid salary of $50,000 per year, the benefits package could be worth an additional $15,000 making the full remuneration, $65,000 per year. Are the benefits you are paying for really worth $15,000 per year or more? Probably not, since many of us don't have the need to use the full benefits package. For instance, some employees never get sick; don't take holidays, or use prescription drugs, may not require glasses, and have excellent dental heath already, don't buy stock options, or contribute to a 401K or RRSP and so on. Consequently these employees are paying for the benefits package anyway. As an employee you are forced to take a lower wage because of the total remuneration package regardless if you want it or not, or if you use it or not, since it's mandatory.

UNION STUFF

Of course, a union environment has some benefits such as, protecting its members from unfair treatment related to pension, wages, work hours, health, safety, training, wrongful dismissals and other work related issues.

With union protection also comes, workplace drawbacks, for those employees who want more from the employer. Those who would like to have more pay, better options, opportunities, and career advancement. All of these are not possible in a union environment. The reason is any sort of opportunity for anyone is given to those who have worked there the longest and have the most seniority, if they're qualified or not.

I recall when it came to holidays; I would have to wait to choose my holiday days. Finally when it was my turn, there really wasn't much left since I was only able to choose from October and November. This wasn't a good time for camping or any other good weather stuff.

Moreover, I couldn't work the day shift with everyone else or the afternoon shift but had to go to midnights or grave yard shift, 11:00 pm to 7:00 am. I couldn't move to another shift, unless someone with higher seniority chose to work midnights for some reason, quit point blank or died before I could actually work day shift. Also, even if any of these situations did happen there was always someone else with more seniority regardless if they worked in the same city or not. In other words, I was stuck on midnight shift for years or possibly decades.

There is also another catch to being unionized, which entails going on strike. This is when all union members stop work and form a line outside the company to protest about something that the union feels is unfair or needs. Usually these union disputes are in regard to wages, benefits, pension plans and so on. However, during a strike, union members lose their full wage and some receive a supplementary payment while others don't. So losing wages because someone or some people decide to go on strike is a disadvantage. Also, many of the members don't want to go on strike and have no awareness of the strike but show-up against their wishes anyway. Keep in mind that strikes can last for years or the company can even close down.

For instance, an article by the Wall Street Journal clearly explains the effects union strikes can have where no one wins and everyone loses. The article, called " Hostess Closes Plants as Workers Strike" states that "Three days of labor strikes have prompted Hostess Brands Inc. to close three plants and mull a possible liquidation of the beleaguered baking company." This is only one example in regard to the negative impact a strike can have. If you would like to read this article, go to the following URL:

www.wsj.com/articles/SB10001424127887324439804578
114862262799942

Another point is I found that many people choose union employment so they can hide from real jobs, do minimal work, get paid, and cannot get fired. Additionally, these are employees who are very inefficient, have low productivity, are carefree that are protected and paid regardless of their output, attitude, looks, drug and alcohol addictions, psychological problems or other things. These people are what non-union based company employees would call, "dead wood." These dead wood types in non-union environments would get fired instead of being retained.

So, if you are an employee working with these dead wood types and have high efficiency, do an excellent job, are professional, highly productive, keen, an idea generated, organizer, and team player, it doesn't matter. Since you are paid like the next person regardless of performance. Besides that "dead wood" will become your supervisor eventually. To put this another way, you get paid the same as Mary, Bill or Joe that do the minimal amount of work, only bitch and complain, create problems and use the protection of the union to the fullest extent they possibly can and keep screwing everything up all the time and don't care.

The only thing dividing you from them is your pride, performance, quality of work, self-worth and self-image. So, how can someone be happy knowing that this actually exists while getting paid the same as others who are entirely different with negative attitudes that just create trouble? It's called union! Also, if the company decided to downsize its union employee size you will get laid off while they stay employed.

TRAINING

Most employers provide training for their employees with internal or external courses, that are online, eLearning or in classroom. The employer will cover costs only for training that pertains to enhancing the employee's knowledge; skill sets or for certifications as long as it is relative to the employee's job. Some employers pay for training their employees are pursuing that is outside of the standard courses being offered by the company. Before the company agrees to pay for such training courses or certifications, the employer will set up contract obligations with their employees. One of the obligations set by the company is to have the employee guarantee they will work for the employer for a set term after they have successfully completed the training.

For instance, an employee wants to take a course on supply chain management or a six sigma black-belt for a certification and have it paid by the company. The company sets up a contract obligation whereby the employee must work for the company for at least 2 years after successfully obtaining the certificate.

This contract obligation is set up by the employer to ensure their employee stays and applies the new acquired skills in their current position and prevent them from running to another company for more pay with their new acquired skills and certification.

Another contractual obligation the employer may require is a minimum average passing grade of 80 percent or more. If the minimum grade requirement is met or exceeded, the employer will pay for the courses. However, if they fail to achieve this then the employee must pay back the company for the course cost in full or via paycheck deductions. On the other hand, if the employee paid the course costs upfront then the employee will have to personally absorb the costs.

These contract terms are put in place to provide drive and incentive for the employee. However, when the company pays for the employee's courses, the costs will be added to the employee's income tax statement, as a taxable benefit found on tax forms W-2 in the USA, T4 in Canada and a P60 in the UK.

This means at year end, the course cost is added to the employee's salary, having the employee pay any required taxes. On the other hand, if the employee personally paid for the education, they may   include this as a personal income tax deduction. The training provider or institute must provide a tax receipt for income tax purposes. Also be aware that the IRS, CRA and HMRC place restrictions on what kind of personal income tax claims are allowable for education, tuition and textbooks and so on. So it's up to you to do your own due diligence. One more point about training is it's always up to the employee's manager or supervisor to decide which courses the employee can take. Generally, employees are only allowed to take courses that are directly in alignment with their current job and this is also dependent on their work schedule and availability. Therefore, if there is a conflict with course time and work schedule, the employee's request for training is rejected.

Another aspect about training deals with an employee wishing to change jobs by adding new skills unrelated to their current position or are courses that are career changing in nature. Most times these types of courses do not align with the company criteria and are declined. The reason is the supervisor or manager may feel that they are, irrelevant, do not add value to the employee's current position or the employee would use the training to transfer to another department.

In other words, in these circumstances the employees are stuck in the same job, even though the courses do benefit the company and employee. As a result employees will have to pay for the course on their own. Additionally, if the employee is trying to make a career change even within the company it is still quite difficult in most circumstances because, most major career changing courses are held at universities or colleges that require daily in class attendance during work hours like 8 am to 4 pm. Many courses are offered on line but overall it becomes very difficult to complete courses due to time restrictions, finances or personal obligations thus becoming another dead end for the employee.

ADDITIONAL BENEFITS

Additional benefits or sometimes called "fringe" benefits an employee may receive could be training, company car, golf membership, cell phone, tablet or car allowance and so on. Fringe benefits at first seem like an awesome perk, but that is only until you find out that they are deemed as a taxable benefit by the HMRC, IRS and CRA.

The employer must add the cost of these benefits to the employee's yearly income tax statement and these benefits are all taxed accordingly. Generally, the amount that is added to your income is money that has not been taxed, and may result in pushing the employee into a higher tax bracket. Meanwhile, the employee usually has no awareness of this benefit being added to their total income.

So what commonly happens is that after the employees taxes are complete they get a wonderful surprise from their accountant stating, "You owe $8000 on your taxes, sorry but that's how the numbers crunched out for last year." This means that the employee must pay the income tax bill to the IRS, CRA or HMRC. Then of course, the employee's response to this is, "WTF is that? 8000 bucks I thought I was getting a refund? How did this happen and where am I going to get 8 grand?"

The amounts added to the employee's income tax statement will vary and correspond to what kind of benefit it is. I have found that vehicles or company cars/trucks that are used fulltime by the employee for both personal and business is one of the largest and quite expensive. Especially if the company pays for all expenses for the vehicle such as insurance, fuel, maintenance and repairs. Also some golf memberships can be very expensive as well as training courses as I mentioned in the prior section. As a rule of thumb the more cost an extra benefit has the more the employee will pay the tax man.

In Canada for company vehicles there are two components used to calculate the tax benefit amount, the standby charge and the operating cost benefit. The standby charge is derived by 2% of the original vehicles market value, plus sales tax and another calculation for length of time the vehicle is available to the employee which is represented by months.

For example, an employee has a company truck with a total market value of $60,000 including tax, which is used for field service and personal use. The vehicle is available 12 months a year because the employee drives it for both business and personal and parks it at home every night. So the calculation for standby charge would be:

Standby Charge is equal to:

2% X ORIGINAL VALUE OF VEHICLE + TAXES X MONTHS AVAILABLE

Or,

.02 x $60,000 x 12 = $14,400

After arriving at a standby charge $14,400, an operating expense benefit is calculated.

The operating cost benefit has two different calculation methods. One method accounts for flat kilometer charges of $0.26 cents per kilometer and the other is choosing half the standby charge. For example, to calculate the operating cost amount we use the flat kilometer charge and 23,000 personal kilometers. The kilometer use is based on less than 50% personal use. The calculation for the total operating cost is:

Total Operating cost = 23,000 x $0.26 = $5980.00

For the total amount of taxable benefit the employee is taxed is:

Total Benefit is equal to:

Standby Charge + Operating Expense Benefit

=$14,400 + $5980

=$20,380

In this case the employer would add $20,380 to the employee's income on top of the regular salary of $70,000. The salary and taxable benefit brings the total income amount to $90,300. However, the employee has only paid tax on $70,000 with regular deductions and the amount of tax required for a $90,300 income is what the employee must pay to the CRA. In this case the difference the employee will pay is about $10,000 to the CRA...surprise!

To find out more information go to the following URLs:

In Canada,

http://www.cra-arc.gc.ca/automotor-benefits/

For some fun use the online CRA Automobile Benefits Calculator at the following URL:

http://www.cra-arc.gc.ca/autobenefits-calculator/

In the US, a company car or vehicle is also taxed accordingly. The method used is based on personal usage of the car as compared to business usage. If the employee uses the car 45% of the time for personal use then this is multiplied by the market value of the vehicle of $40,000. So the total fringe benefit for this company vehicle would calculate as follows:

Personal Usage Percentage x Car Cost

=.45 x $40,000

=$18,000

The employee in this circumstance would have a fringe benefit of $18,000 added to their income tax statement and taxed accordingly.

For more information about fringe benefits go to the following URLs:

https://www.irs.gov/publications/p15b/ar02.html

http://smallbusiness.chron.com/calculate-imputed-income-company-car-20112.html

However, in the UK the calculations are more complex because of breaking down specifics about the company vehicle, which includes, the manufacturer, model, engine size, fuel type, trim, year and plate, tax year and tax rate.

For more information regarding a company car benefit in the UK go to the following URLS:

https://www.gov.uk/calculate-tax-on-company-cars

https://www.gov.uk/tax-company-benefits/tax-on-company-cars

Or have some fun by using this company car calculator.

http://www.parkers.co.uk/company-cars/tax-calculator/

The whole idea about additional benefits is that the employee is taxed because of the personal component or usage.

Again, it is very important to do your own due diligence by asking an accountant or calling your local tax preparer, CRA, IRS or HMRC offices to find out what the consequences are of taking on these benefits. They may seem wonderful at the time, until you realize you are paying for them at tax time. I feel that this surprise of paying a huge tax bill is a total disadvantage.

THE COMMUTE

Employees commute on a daily basis from home to work and return. Some of the fortunate people live in close proximity to their workplace while others are faced with lengthy commutes via car, rail, bus or taxi. When it comes to commuting, there are a few factors to strongly consider like, the time it takes to commute, lost time and cost.

Commute and Lost Time

When it comes to actual commute time, an employee may work in the city center; work in a suburb or even a small rural town just outside a main city. Employees driving to work are faced with extended commute times because of situations such as, rush hour traffic, accidents, traffic jams, parking congestion, road conditions, weather conditions and construction. Therefore, employees must tolerate a return commute that may take one to three hours or more.

For instance, if the employee works from 8:00 am to 4:00 pm, then we can assume personal time is from 4:00 pm to midnight to do any personal stuff. In other words, an employee only has eight hours of personal time on workdays, if that.

Hence, if the commute is based on a range of 1 to 3 hours per day, and 22 working days per month, then each month the employee loses a range of 22 to 66 personal time hours per month. If we consider 8 hours of personal time to be defined as a personal day, it suggests when calculating this, that the employee can lose, 3 to 9 personal days per month.

If we extrapolate a little further and calculate for an entire year, then the accumulated lost personal time on the low end of the scale is, 22 hours x 12 equaling 264 hours. On the high end of the scale of lost personal time, if we calculate 66 hours x 12 equaling 792 hours. Therefore, lost personal time ranges from 264 to 792 hours per year or 33 to 99 personal days per year or from 1 to 3 months per year. Some food for thought to mention that is even more shocking is... what if we add all this personal lost time over the employee's entire work life of 40 years.

This Is Time Gone...Never To Be Recovered Ever!

Commute Costs

When an employee uses their car for commuting, costs rise for fuel, maintenance and repairs, then add in additional wear and tear, high mileage as well as having no car to use because of repair downtime. These result in degrading the reliability of the car, increasing the age and condition of the car, while drastically reducing its value. For example, when the car value is significantly reduced it could mean that the employee is paying a car loan for a $20,000 car while it's only worth $9,000. As a permanent employee all car expenses cannot be claimed as an income tax expense making the employee personally eat the costs.

However, if the employee decides not to drive and reduces commute costs by using alternative methods instead such as, light rail transit, bus, or taxi, the employee is still paying out of pocket expenses which again cannot be claimed as an expense on their income tax. Moreover, by using different types of transportation the employee may be extending the commute time thus losing more personal time or may even cut travel time. Cutting travel time can happen but overall it may make no difference due to train, transit or utility equipment failures, accidents, equipment maintenance and other delays.

Also, when the employee is paying for travel to and from the work location it is paid for by the employee using their net income. This is like paying another tax on top of the taxes they have already paid because they are using their NET pay. The cost to commute to the job location is all very costly any way you slice it. Commute costs can add up to a hundreds of dollars per year or more.

For instance, if an employee drives a round trip of 30 miles to work each day then if we extrapolate by using 22 working days per month. The calculation is 22 x 30 equaling 660 miles per month or 7920 miles per year. Note that this mileage is only for work and doesn't include mileage for shopping, travel, appointments and other personal usage.

Consequently, the longer the commute time, the more costly it is and increases the amount of lost personal time. Gee, I wonder why we don't have time during the week to do a lot of things like fix the fence, go for dinner, go to a movie, grocery shopping, take a course, learn a new language, and so on. A final note is this doesn't factor in extra work time employees have to put in, due to job demands and deadlines, reducing personal time even more. This actually reminds me of a story about commuting when I was a Technical Manager.

Coffee to Go

As a manager I would commute but also would quite frequently drive round trip twice a day. This would mean that I would be driving 40 miles per day and when being called in for problems would increase the mileage to 80 miles per day. I estimate that total mileage was around 300 to 350 miles per week or roughly 1200 to 1600 miles per month. These were miles I could not claim on my income tax, nor the fuel cost or the wear and tear on my car. At the time I didn't care much since I was driving a four door Reliant K car that had a small 4 cylinder motor with over 250,000 miles on it and still had excellent fuel economy.

Driving 20 miles to work would give me enough time to grab a large black coffee at a drive-thru coffee shop before embarking to work. Every morning I would drink a large coffee and throw the empty paper cup into the back seat area. This continued for over 6 months until I was shockingly pulled over by the police.

I couldn't believe that I was pulled over since I wasn't driving erratically or speeding or breaking any laws. Puzzled, I rolled down my window and waited for the police officer. The officer stood at my driver's side window and I could see him look into the back seat area.

Then he asked, "Can I see your driver's license and insurance?" I immediately handed it over. He went back to his car to check my registration and that everything was in order.

He started to approach the car and I could see him glancing at the back seat area. He handed back all of my paper work and while looking into the back seat area he asked, "Do you travel a lot?" I was sort of confused with the question but said, "Yes I do, travel every day because I live in main city and work in the small city just down the highway." Then I saw him look into the back seat again. So I asked, "Why do you ask about travel?"

After I asked I knew...it was the coffee cups that filled the entire back seat area that were almost pouring into the front seat. Then with laughter I said, "Oh shit I get it...all those coffee cups in the back seat right?" He smiled and said, "Yes I just thought I would ask." Then I asked, "Is there a problem officer because I wasn't speeding or anything and feel sort of confused why I would be pulled over." He said, "Your plate sticker has expired" and I replied with concern, "Oh my God, expired aren't they supposed to send a notification?" He said, "Yes unless you recently moved." I replied, "Oh shit, yes I did recently move about 5 months ago." He said okay that makes sense." I curiously asked, "How expired is my plate a couple weeks? Then he replied," Try six months." I responded, "Oh, oh now what?" The officer said, "I'll tell you what, you update your plate registration, go to the local police station with this slip I am giving you and show proof of registration and you'll be good to go, no fine but get this done as soon as you can." I took a deep breath smiled and said, "Thanks for the break officer I'll do that immediately." Note that an unregistered vehicle could be towed on the spot while you find a way to get back home.

PARKING

Parking usually is not an issue for employees that don't drive to work or when parking is paid for or provided by the employer. The employer pays for or provides parking only if the employer is located in a suburb, in a small rural town outside the main city or a location outside the city core like in an industrial area and so on.

However, when the employer is located in the downtown area, companies do not pay for employee parking. Actually throughout my experiences I have never had an employer cover parking costs in the downtown area which can be very expensive ranging from $200 to $1000 per month.

This all depends on the city and the location in the city. Parking costs are not considered as an employment expense, so the employee cannot claim this deduction on their personal income tax even though the employee again uses their NET pay to pay for another type of indirect tax called parking.

SALARY CLUSTER

Another disadvantage I have experienced stems from being a salaried employee. Companies generally calculate salaries by using working days over a one year period, then to arrive at a monthly salary and an hourly rate. This is calculated over an annual period because each year will have variations in how many working days there are due to statutory and public holiday placement. For example, in the US, in 2015 there were 240 working days while in 2016 there is 251 working days. With that in mind, some salaried employees who work overtime time hours are paid time and half or double time while other salaried employees are not paid for any overtime or extra hours.

An employee being paid overtime hours is up to the company and its policies, even though the employer has to abide by local, state, provincial or federal labor laws. Be aware that when an employee is hired, the employee usually signs an employment agreement which may override some labor laws. I am not going to explore government labor laws since it is beyond the scope of this book.

Nonetheless, there are companies that do not pay their employees any overtime instead they are paid their regular salary, with no extra pay or time off in lieu. Salaried employees are expected to work any hours required by their employer, in order to get the job done, regardless of the day, the time or amount of hours they put in.

Companies justify this type of salaried practice mainly by a tradeoff of paid floater days an employee receives which the employer feels will cover any accrued overtime. This may seem fair but what happens when the company you work for doesn't have any floater days or the extra hours worked exceeds the amount of floaters days? As a salaried employee, the employee has no choice because this is part of their employment agreement they signed. Therefore, it is in the best interest of the employee to do their own due diligence to ensure they know exactly what they are signing.

Another point is, when an employee works overtime hours they are compensated by being paid, time and half or double time. The reason is the employee works outside of regular work hours, using their personal time. However, when a salaried employee works overtime they are actually trading overtime hours for regular hour since floater days are regular pay. Is this situation fair? Sure it is, for the employer, not for the employee.

I was fortunate enough to experience this salaried employee kind of stuff first hand. I recall at my first salaried employment, that I didn't understand what I was getting into. The salary was, paid every month, but it was broken-down to a mid-month paycheck which was considered an advance, and it was usually a smaller amount than the end of the month paycheck. Nonetheless, I thought this was excellent especially when

I saw the salary amount because it was the most I was ever paid as an employee.

Life was great, huge salary, however I had no idea what was coming next. I didn't care much about anything because I assumed that the amount of hours that I would put in, would work out with the amount of salary I was getting paid, besides the salary was ginormous!

At this supervisor job, I first started working 5 days a week in the shop from 8 am to 5 pm. After some training I was shifted out to the field. At that point, I realized that the hours I worked were changing and started to ramp up. In fact, it turned out that this wonderful salary that I was receiving when calculated out on an hourly basis turned out to be significantly reduced. This is how it played out.

As a simple example, usually employees will work anywhere from 37 to 44 hours per week, which is considered a normal range. So if the employee is paid $20 per hour it equates to roughly $41,600 per annum, $3,467 per month or $800 per 40 hour work week based on 5 days per week, 8 hours a day. Keep in mind that each company has their own method of calculating salary for their employees. When a salaried employee not paid for overtime starts to work more than the base hours per week this suddenly reduces their hourly calculated rate because their salary amount remains the same.

In my personal example, I was working 14 to 16 hours a day in the field, 7 days a week. This on the low end works out to 14 x 7 or 98 hours per week and on the high end 16 x 7 or 112 hours per week. If I use the $800 per week salary amount, it's not a $20 per hour job anymore. The reason is I was not working 40 hours per week but instead a range of 98 to 112 hours. When using the same salary amount and the increased work hours to calculate the hourly rate it's not $20 per hour, but substantially reduced to 800 divided by 98 or 112 to arrive at an hourly rate range of $7.14 to $8.16 per hour. This to my surprise was less than half of the pay that I agreed to. I can't emphasize this enough, do your own due diligence and find out what you are actually signing.

After experiencing a salaried employee position like this one, I made it mandatory, to either work for an hourly rate or if being paid a salary that it is still calculated at an hourly rate and to be paid overtime rates of time and a half. Every salaried position I was offered that didn't pay overtime, I without hesitation outright refused.

TRAVEL TIME

Travel time to and from various work locations may not seem to be an issue especially if there is no travel involved with the employee's current job. However, when employees travel as a part of their job, companies usually do not pay for any extra time the employee travels, outside their regular work hours. Travel time for employees is not covered since employers feel that this is a part of their job, covered by their benefits and floater days. Does this trade-off of floater days sound familiar?

For instance, I recall travelling to a northern city to attend a full day meeting. A colleague and I, after working from 7:00 am to 3:00 pm, drove to the location arriving at the hotel, after 7:00 pm. This was unpaid time and amounted to 4 hours of overtime. The next day we attended the meeting which ran from 8:00 am to 4:00 pm then left to return home. While driving back, there was an accident that shut down the highway and delayed our return until the accident was cleared. This return trip normally would take about 4 hours but with the accident it took us an additional 2 hours so we didn't get back until 10:00 pm. This was another 6 hours of overtime to add to the trip, making it a total of 10 hours of overtime that the company would not pay for.

If we do some simple calculations for this loss of 10 hours of overtime and multiply it by 1.5 it equals 15 hours of regular time. This is almost equivalent to two full floater days. Hey, I thought floater days were supposed to be an advantage for employees!

Another example, was while working for an international service company, we were flying to locations all over the world. The field support crew of 4 to 5 employees would travel to their locations but never get paid for the time spent travelling. One way travel time could range from 8 hours to a couple of days.

If you do the math and calculate this for a whole year this adds up to weeks of unpaid travel time. This situation was in my opinion completely unreasonable and I discussed it with the manager of operations. I wrote a complete report of existing field related problems and their solutions. When presenting this report to the manager of operations he clearly understood the problems and the tension it was creating with all field staff.

In turn, the manager distributed this report to the CEO and other senior management to successfully change the current situation. The changes were, to pay for travel based on a flat daily rate, as well as, introducing a pay multiplier for each country of origin. The multiplier was based on the countries living conditions, length of stay, instability, and level of risk. It was a common practice to be in countries for at least 2 to 3 months at any one time.

At least in this circumstance I was able to change the pay structure for many of the field operational aspects of the company, but most times companies don't change their policies and unfortunately, have the "take it or leave it" attitude. So, travel time results in a substantial amount of hours that are unpaid which can be a very significant financial loss for the employee especially if the travel frequency is high. This by far is a clear disadvantage for the employee. Have you ever lived out of a suitcase for more than a week or two? It gets old very quickly.

WEALTH EFFECT

Wealth effect is about people, who become wealthy, and it doesn't matter where in the world they live, nor does it have any bearing on how many kids or children they have, what kind of childhood they experienced, education level, age, gender, the position they hold or the pay they receive.

First of all, wealthy doesn't mean someone who has a big house or drives a Mercedes or Porsche. Since, those may be people who make enough money and spend it all making payments, so they don't really own anything. This is not real wealth but only appears that way.

On the other hand, wealthy people do not make purchases like buying huge houses, extravagant cars, and depreciating assets unless they are extremely wealthy. The wealthy, buy moderate sized houses don't focus on purchases, like the latest gadgets, and need stuff; their focus is on living their life with family and close friends. They also are frequently looking for financial opportunities. However, middle class employees have a different focus in regard to money, buying and needing stuff.

Generally, employees focus on comfort and safety as I discussed earlier which equates to having it as easy as possible, by having a secure job, and working for someone else. When you are an employee, it means that, you are not going to become wealthy.

The reason is that the salary or hourly wage the employee receives when working in a union or other jobs are within the lower middle to middle class income range. This means that many employees are neither rich nor poor, but instead are comfortable. Also, employees are generally set up in the main stream of minimal savings because three quarters of their wealth is tied up in the value of their homes, and there is more to the picture.

Middle range income earners also take on long-term debt, to fall right into the "buy now and pay later' scheme that actually fits into most employee's way of thinking. According to a Bloomberg View article which states, "As of 2013, the average debt of middle-class families -- those that fall within the middle three-fifths of the population by earnings -- amounted to an estimated 122 percent of annual income, according to the Federal Reserve."

If you are interested in more information about consumer debt, check out the Federal Reserve report website at:

http://www.federalreserve.gov/econresdata/scf/scfindex.htm

Commonly, middle range income earners are shopaholics, taking on debt related to stuff they don't really need since they like to show off, and are generally in competition with the Johnson's or their other neighbors, the Kirfuknicks.

These middle income earners tend to live way above their means by buying huge houses, and cottages. Moreover, they are in an endless chase to have and possess the latest toys and technology. During their pursuit for goods they spend money on items such as, depreciating assets like cars, fifth wheels, campers, cell phones, tablets, televisions, surround sound systems, gaming systems, and other toys. The employees also can't have basic cable but want a full cable package and the highest speed internet access available. Shortly after, the depreciating assets are sold for a fraction of the cost to buy the newer model or thrown in the garbage or are passed on to some charity. Keep in mind that giving to any reputable charity or cause is always a good thing.

Of course these same people ask and wonder why they aren't wealthy. It's clearly because they have a different focus than the real wealthy do. Hey, don't get me wrong here since I am not being judgmental. People must do what works for them. Besides, there are always exceptions for example, some standup, change their mindset and focus on wealth building but most do not. This cycle of paying bills and adding more toys, then paying more bills is detrimental to employees and they never really acquire any real wealth but only debt and toys that lose value.

This is clearly a disadvantage in my opinion because the wealth effect I am discussing is based on employee mindset and the heart of it is safety. With safety there is no risk therefore no chance of taking any risk that may have a life changing outcome. Why do you think millionaires and billionaires are wealthy? They take risks.

BIG GUARANTEES

Employees generally believe in a few guarantees, a regular paycheck, their job and pension. After working as an employee for public, private and government unionized companies, I have formed some different views and thoughts about job and pension guarantees.

Employees feel that being in a permanent job working for a private, public, non-union or union company is an advantage and secure. However, they don't realize that they can be released or fired just as easily as any consultant or contractor or in fact can be released before a temporary worker, contractor or consultant.

The difference between how secure the union and non-union permanent employee's job is, boils down to two simple things. First the employee working for a non-union company can be fired by the employer for any reason or even "no reason" at all but cannot fire the employee for any reason that is discriminatory or retaliatory in nature.

The second is in regard to a union employee getting fired, which is a little more difficult but can be done successfully as long as the employer has handled the situation correctly. By this, the employer is compliant with the collective agreement, and any governing and arbitral legislation. Additionally, by following the correct routes employers also have the right to downsize their current unionized workforce size at any time.

In truth, union or non-union, no employee is exempt from losing their job nor guaranteed a job. The end result usually is the employee receives a compensation package and must pay tax on it. However if they don't receive a package or it's a wrongful dismissal the employee will usually seek legal counsel and establish a law suit against the company for wrongful dismissal. This results in the company paying a lump sum which goes to the lawyer, who gets paid very well and to the employee, and then it's over. So, even after the litigation, and arbitration the employee has still lost their job regardless.

I found out about guarantees the hard way while working for a large non-union company. This is a personal example of mine when I was a Technical Manager for a large field service company. I use this example because it clearly shows the, ruthless, calculated, carefree, and sociopathic behaviors of senior management and how employees may be treated. This is one example of my experiences about guarantees and this is when I changed my beliefs and mindset.

It all started when I was approached by an oilfield service company that was having loads of field operations problems. After being approached several times by a friend who worked there as a sales rep, I decided to accept the technical manager position. I agreed to take on this efficiency improvement adventure which I believed would advance my career but also mostly to help a friend. My friend's sales world was crumbling due to operational failures and nightmares, resulting from the company's market share slowly collapsing and the company losing $2 million a month in revenue.

At the time this company didn't pose as competition to other companies since its operational efficiency was around 40 percent if that. So in other words, every time they attempted to provide field service they would have a gong show and get run off the work location by the client. In turn the client would immediately replace this company with a competing company that was in the vicinity that had the ability to efficiently perform the same services. This kind of situation made it clear that, efficiency problems required some exploration.

After working for three months at this company and performing analysis, I was of course shocked with the findings and it all made sense. No wonder this company was failing at almost every service they performed. Upon completing my failure analysis, the operations manager announced that I would be the new Technical Manager and taking over the repair, maintenance and lab group. After this I had several general meetings with all staff to announce the future changes I would be making to improve the operational efficiencies. I also would conduct small meetings with field engineers and the technical staff to explain the benefits of my strategies and how the processes I created would be applied and used.

In addition to the changes, a bonus system was also introduced to all technical lab staff which was based on operational efficiency levels, for example: at 60% operational efficiency a bonus of 60% of the employee's salary would be paid, at 70%, 70 % is paid and so on. This in fact was a huge carrot and driver the technical staff had in place, because bonus was extra money on top of salary, and overtime.

With the research about the company's operations in hand, I went full speed ahead with a plan. I started to write a number of memos to a point where people started calling me "memo man". These were the first step to putting procedures and some controls in place for operational maintenance and repairs. I created and implemented forms to be filled out by shop and field staff to make measurements in the system. This was to generate some metrics so I could have a look at where we are now, develop a baseline and then to monitor our progress.

A couple of weeks later, I had a meeting with the operations manager to inform him that I required two additional staff. The first person I hired was a past co-worker to join our team since he knew the path to bring us to excellence. The next day I hired my ex-coworker, Barry Jones, got him a good base salary and he joined the team within two weeks. For the second person, I had HR run an ad then within two weeks I began interviewing potential candidates. I found almost everyone seemed to lack the enthusiasm, drive, and knowledge I was looking for. Then I interviewed, Brenda Bates, who was a tech graduate was driven, bright, very willing to learn and to join the team. I hired her, as I felt she was a keener and in the end my intuition was correct.

My staff and I were making substantial changes that transformed all the old operational processes into new efficient ones. As a rule of thumb, with any kind of change people usually start to feel fear and it creates anxiety. To try and ease the anxiety, I would put on training presentations to explain what we are doing, why and how we are changing things to get to our end goal and how it benefits everyone. Of course, these were changes that many current employees didn't like regardless of how you explained it. I found it really didn't make any difference since I was dealing with many old school employees that were there for over 20 years doing the same thing. Their mindset was, "Why fix something when it isn't broke?" as they perceived of the company's performance.

Even after providing multiple information seminars and Q&A sessions, it was still an uphill battle all the way with very few people on the positive side of change. Nonetheless, my staff and I continued to push the company into the right direction and to a different level of operation and service. As time progressed, I tackled many design flaws in some of the instruments which were a large part of the equipment failures and finally started to see operational efficiencies slowly rise. The lab and field staff started to acknowledge that operations were changing to the positive, as equipment failure was being reduced, in turn raising people's confidence. They started to have hope and confidence in their equipment and the support staff. This was the most satisfying for me. They were amazed and thrilled at the turning point. After a long, grueling and tedious fight this was finally coming to fruition, we were all on our way, since the trend had distinctly changed.

The operational efficiencies continued on their journey upward and people started to recognize the impact that the team and I had made. People didn't fight change anymore but welcomed it. The lab staff was pleased when they started to get bonuses which kicked in at 60% efficiency while the field engineers were making more money because the equipment and operational efficiencies were reliable. The field engineer's bonus was coming in at full force, as it should have, years ago.

Everything started to fall in to place just as I had expected, and the biggest payoff was to have people experience first-hand, the real tangible proof of the effects and results of changes that were made. Failures were becoming a thing of the past and a new future was taking hold. This paved a clear path of confidence that swept throughout the field, lab staff, and owners of the company. The time, effort and plan put in place to stabilize operations, correct engineering design problems, and lab procedures turned out to be very effective. So effective that it gave this company a long overdue face-lift.

Efficiencies continued to climb and there was no forecast only real numbers. It continued to increase month by month, and after 9 months we were sitting at over ninety percent operational efficiency. I was proud of the team for helping me achieve what I was hired to do. This was a huge, stressful and painful undertaking that took, many hours of overtime, frustration, fighting and arguing with people, as well as, introducing innovating ideas and business analysis acumen and problem solving. Yes, I stood proud because what I set out to do actually surpassed the level that I envisioned. After a long and tedious road I was on top of the world. I bought a new car, the first new car I had ever owned since I felt great with the achievements, felt confident in my job outlook and secure in my position. I received a letter of praise from the CEO and from the Manager of Research and Development. So here I was on top of the world just after 12 months of being there…but at the same time there were other things happening in my personal life.

On the personal side of things, my mother at 62, found out she had bowel cancer and it was far too advanced and was given two weeks to live.

Nonetheless, she continued with chemo therapy which kept her alive for 2 more years but according to her, it only gave her one day a month of feeling good. This went on until her passing. She passed, and my father was devastated by the loss of his soul mate of over 40 years. He setup her funeral and had her body placed in a mausoleum. I had taken a couple days off work to attend her funeral. Completely devastated, I went to her funeral and was overwhelmed with pain, loss, grief, and anguish, wondering why this would happen to someone like her at the age of 64. She, never smoked, drank just worked hard and loved her children. After attending her funeral that Friday, I returned to work the following Monday morning.

Professionally, I was on top of the world but devastated on the personal front with the loss of my mother. That morning I focused on my job since, that was the only positive thing I had in my life. After working about an hour or so, the operations manager asked me to come to his office to talk. At 9:30 am, I walked up the stairs and sat down in his office, looking at him, thinking that he was going to express his condolences about the loss of my mother but it wasn't the case.

He looked at me with a blank expression and said, "After some review, I find that you don't fit into the business model or the company anymore so I am letting you go." I was confused. Then after a few seconds I responded in anger, "What! You are getting rid of me after all of the stuff that I have done here, that I accomplished for this company, the stress and frustrations and anxiety! All the crap I have put up with fighting and arguing with people" I continued, "You can't do this to me this is a wrongful dismissal!" The manager said, "Ah…Please grab your things if you have anything here and the safety manager will escort you out, thanks."

Can you believe it, fired, no severance package or anything just fired on the spot, with no notice. What happened to all the things I did for this company? After all the time, effort, frustrations, disappointments and anguish I went through to achieve and deliver this level of operational efficiency then to only be thrown away like a worthless piece of garbage.

On top of it all, this bomb was dropped two days after my mother's funeral. Immediately questions started to go through my head like, what kind of a company was I working for that would do this? What kind of cold hearted people are these? How could I work for people like this? Why did I do this for such people who just used and exploited me? All this hard work for their benefit, what did I gain? I thought that if they did the same thing to someone else, that person might return to the workplace but with a gun to take care of business. Me, I would never do something like that.

After all of that effort, I finally achieved a 95% efficiency level which in turn, created an incredibly recognizable facelift to the company. In other words, when a company has current efficiencies levels of 90 percent and they rise to 95% there is not much of a noticeable difference. However, when you are at an operational efficiency of 40% to jump to 95% within 12 months, this is a huge contrast and extremely noticeable. Past clients were shocked by an enormous turnaround in the company's operational efficiencies and this created a massive increase in market share, competitive edge, creating tens of millions of dollars in new and future contracts. Clients were instilled with confidence, because a whole new image of the company was created.

I, on the other hand, felt devastated by my mother's death and about being fired. Now I was feeling, angry, heartbroken, disappointed, and betrayed. This made me feel worthless, unwanted and unworthy of other jobs. I was also worried about losing my first brand new car, from defaulting on car loan payments now that I didn't have a job.

After a while, I eventually stood up and pursued the company for a wrongful dismissal but the lawyer I hired took advantage of my anger. In the end the lawyer received $7,000 and I got $8,000 for the wrongful dismissal. So after all of that, what was it all worth? It was worth nothing. This only proves that any person regardless of their position, union or non-union, can be like one of those disposable staff as you see on Star-trek or other TV shows. In truth, companies can fire you for whatever reason they feel, if any and the ramifications are nothing.

The truth is, for the company, to pay an employee off with $20,000 or even $50,000 means nothing to them, because they move on while the employee's life is shattered. Sure I received many letters of praise from the owners of the company, CEO, and Manager of Research and Development, but it didn't mean anything in the end, because it was all for their benefit and the company's not mine. This company's facelift produced millions of dollars of new revenue. All I received was a small payment to achieve a huge undertaking. Was it worth it for me? Would I ever do this again? Never!

All of this was chalked up as experience of being used and exploited. I came to the conclusion that after I achieved the level the company wanted I was no longer an asset to them. So, I packed up and moved south to another city, to a new life. So do I believe there is a guarantee in being an employee? I don't see any especially after this experience. My beliefs were completely shattered and in the end, it changed another part of my beliefs and my employee mind-set.

All I know about the people that did this to me is...

Karma's a bitch!

DON'T MOVE

Yes, don't move, hop or bounce around please. You should stay put. Well you may be a bit confused, and wondering what it is I am talking about. The point I am raising here is about aggressive and ambitious employees who are looking for more. These individuals are searching for opportunities like a better job, higher pay, more benefits, better working conditions and a clear path to excel. An employee wanting to improve their status and livelihood is a positive action. However, it isn't a benefit for companies when their employees leave.

Companies focus on employee retention for a number of reasons which are both monetary and intangible. This is why changing employers becomes a disadvantage for employees. Employers want to retain them because of the costs associated with bringing a new hire up to a point of being productive and adding value to the company. This is a big investment for the company that includes HR or agency costs, advertising, interviewing, screening and finally hiring the right candidate and onboarding. Then after hiring, the company continues to provide more training and manage the candidate.

The training and management period can be anywhere from 6 months to 2 years before a new hire's productivity is comparable to that of an existing employee. The monetary costs are up to two years of salary plus any additional training costs over a 24 month period which average at least 25% of their yearly salary.

There are other factors that play a role for employees who stay long term at companies. Employees actually become assets that appreciate, gaining more and more value the longer they stay. The reason being, long term employees reach a sound understanding of the company's big picture. Their experience and knowledge about the company's products and services enhance the company's customer service, reputation, products, services, quality and so on.

Besides the monetary costs of employees who leave, there are other subtle things that make negative impacts which can affect other employees, especially if the employee is unhappy before leaving. A negative attitude can affect and sway the overall morale of many employees, and reduce productivity, since all it takes is one bad apple.

As a result, employers frown upon individuals that frequently change companies because of the monetary and intangible losses. So when companies review a resume or CV that shows a potential candidate is switching jobs frequently, this clearly suggests the individual is inconsistent and unstable. This observation immediately brings up a flag with many concerns and questions, such as,

1. "If we hire this person, how long are they going to stay with our company? It looks like they change companies

every six months, then we have to start the whole process all over again."

2. "Do we want to hire someone who has had 7 jobs in the past five years? This candidate is too much of a risk for our organization since it appears they have no loyalty or stability."

3. "Is this person just going to get some experience and training then go to one of our competitors shortly after for more money? It sure looks like it according to the salary history this person provided."

4. "Think of the costs of time, effort and training it takes to bring a new hire to a productive level. This person will leave at that point, and then we start all over again. Who else is there that we can consider other than this candidate?"

5. "Next, forget this candidate lets hire someone who wants to stay long term and climb our career ladder"

Generally, companies are looking to hire employees who are loyal, stable and consistent who are willing to stay for the long haul. The basic stereotype of stable people that companies are looking for includes individuals who are experienced, mature, married, and have a family.

For example, I was always searching for new jobs. When looking over my resume or CV the employers could clearly see that I would stay in positions for 6 to 36 months then move on. This was clearly a sign of instability and on several occasions I was asked directly, why they should hire me when I am switching jobs all the time.

All I could say was that, I was interested in their position, required work to earn a living and discussed some of the problems and reasons why I had left some past employers. At times, this was enough for many companies but some employers would outright not hire me based on my pattern of jumping from job to job and company to company. However, I felt I had just cause for hopping around and besides I had many reasons not excuses.

As far as the reasons that were propelling me to hop around from company to company all stemmed from details like:

- Being bored

- No path for advancement

- No new opportunities

- No new interests

- No structure or policies in place

- Too much travel

- Completely disorganized company

- Too much overtime

- High stress and anxiety

- Change of the management and management style

- Change of environment

- Company values and my values not aligned

- Poor economic conditions or factors

- Unfair treatment

- Personal problems that arose while employed, that could not be dealt with while employed such as loss of loved one, relationship problems and so on

- Fit at first and after some time didn't fit anymore

- Not fun or interesting anymore

- Have plateaued in knowledge

- Not enough money

- Found better paying jobs

- No salary increases

- Information in interview before taking the job was not the truth

- Many people upset, angry, with very low morale

- Your expectations and their expectations do not align

- Conflict with other coworkers due to coworkers viewing me as a threat instead of a team player

I found the primary reasons for hopping around are generally because of a few main reasons like, the job is a dead end as far as career advancement goes, low wages, not fitting in anymore which is based on values, policies, principles, expectations and so on. The best one and my all-time favorite is what you were told in the interview prior to accepting the job, is totally different from what it really is. This includes, work environment, morale of employees, treatment and other things. This reminds me of an example of having ethics problems with a company.

For example, when I was working for a large electrical company, as an industrial electronics technologist, I was paid well, had a company car and would do service calls around the city on anything that had electronics, like a furnace used for heat treating Boeing aircraft parts, optical coating machines, electroplating machines, or Faulkner F-28 airplane ground power supply units.

The company was privately owned and the president of the company was a blunt, aloof, insensitive, impersonal, money oriented, serious, and cheap person. He lived without any feelings so people were treated accordingly. I didn't know this at the time since I very rarely had any dealings with this person. However, the reason I did find these things out about him was, the situation I heard and witnessed when standing three feet from the conversations.

On this day an employee Gary was an inside sale person for the company for two decades and a really nice fellow. He had a bubbly personality and was quite entertaining. However, I remember him entering the electronics lab, and looked very uncomfortable and holding his abdomen as if he was in deep pain. He blurted out to Allan a senior tech, "Al, you have to drive me to the hospital, there is something seriously wrong with me, because I'm in so much bloody pain!" Allan, immediately told Gary he would do it immediately. So, they left the shop and I...was quite concerned about Gary.

About 15 minutes later the owner came into the lab and asked, "Does anyone know where Allan is?" then James replied, "Allan drove Gary to the hospital emergency and it looked like Gary was in deep pain with some serious problem." The owner didn't say anything he just walked out.

About two hours later, Allan returned without Gary. I asked, "Allan is Gary okay, what happened? Allan replied,

"He had some abdominal problems and went straight into exploratory surgery!" I replied, "Oh wow sounds really serious I sure hope he is okay". Alan said," No worries, he is in good hands, I'm sure they will find out what it is." About 10 minutes later the owner walks in and approaches Allan. The owner immediately asks, "Allan where were you?" and Allen responded, "I drove Gary to the closest Hospital Emergency because he was having some serious problem". The owner coldly replied, "Allan don't ever do that kind of stuff like that again, because you know that we have cheaper labor in the back shop that could have drove him!"

I was about three feet away from the conversation and couldn't believe my ears; it was as if this person wasn't human. Not one molecule of compassion or empathy, I was disgusted, at the thought of working for this cold-hearted a-hole. I stood there thinking about what I wanted to say and it would have sounded something like this, "Just wait you frickin a-hole until you have a heart-attack and I'll be sure to throw you a quarter so you can call yourself a taxi! " Of course I didn't say anything. Shortly after though, I found a job with another company and left immediately, because I couldn't work for someone like this.

Regardless of the reasons, an employee hopping around frequently puts the employee at a disadvantage, because many companies will immediately overlook their resume. Some companies may call you in for an interview because of your experience and to get a feel about your intentions and mindset, but overall they are leery about hiring you.

Other companies may hire you then you leave shortly after, because you will find out the true realities of the company and the environment. In other words, it's like a sweat shop and they should have a revolving front door because of such high employee turnover. As long as you are an employee, and you have many job transitions on your resume and keep jumping around, you are at a full disadvantage.

BENEFITS PACKAGE

I feel that benefits packages are more hype and disadvantages than a benefit. I say this because the reality is benefits are not free. Each employee must pay for their benefits package coverage via monthly deductions off their paycheck.

Another point is geared towards the employee benefits being mandatory. This means that the employee has no choice regardless if they want them or not. So the employee has no choice to choose what benefits or coverage they would like or what insurance company will provide them.

Also, there are restrictions and limitations your benefits provider places on how much you actually can claim on each item of your benefits package. Some examples are vision care, psychological services, physio therapy, massage therapy and so on. Generally benefits coverage is only a fraction of the total cost, usually 20 to 25% and limited to a yearly total claim amount except prescription drugs which have 90% coverage. For example, when using the massage benefit, a one hour massage may cost $90 and the benefits plan will cover $20 of the cost for a total of 12 sessions or $240 per year. Therefore, as an employee, you pay $70 out of pocket per massage. If we look at the costs over a year, benefits pay $240 for 12 sessions while the employee out of pocket expense is $840.

When claiming other benefits, such as dental expenses, there is always a waiting period of 3 months before the benefit is active. Additionally, there are set limits of coverage for crowns, dentures, regular check-ups and cleaning services. For example, the insurance company covers only 50% of the crowns costs and there are also limitations on the yearly claim amount.

In other words, to have a crown installed may cost $1,500 but after benefits are applied, this is reduced to $750 for the employee's out of pocket costs. However, if you add in a cleaning and a checkup, you may have reached the yearly limit for dental coverage. What if you need another crown and you want to use your dental coverage, but have already reached the maximum yearly claim amount. Now you may have to wait until the next year to have the crown work done. Basically, the insurance company is dictating when you will get your dental work done and covered.

What if you can't wait and you need dental work now? The employee will pay out of pocket costs for the full amount. When paying out of pocket dental expenses, only a small portion of the total cost is allowed to be used as a claim on your income tax return. For example, in Canada if the medical expenses you and your family are claiming are eligible according to the CRA, you can claim up to 3% of your total income or $2,208 whichever is lower. Also keep in mind that the CRA, HMRC and IRS have a list of eligible expenses that can be claimed. Note that the total claim amount on the income tax form is not a direct deduction only a fixed and small percentage of it.

Another point to add is the insurance company benefits provider is not going to allow employees to claim amounts that surpass the employee's yearly benefit contribution amount because the insurance company has to make money too. If benefit contributions are being exceeded by the amount employees claim then benefits costs will rise.

This is only a basic example of why benefits are not really a benefit because the amount the employee contributes to the benefit plan is equal to or more than the amount the plan covers. As an employee you are paying out of pocket medical type expenses for most items with NET income which has already been taxed.

GOVERNMENT PENSION CONTRIBUTIONS

Pension contributions for government based pension plans are a disadvantage since there is no real guarantee the funds will exist in the future. Besides, who can make predictions of 30 or 40 years into the future? No one can predict the future only make estimates which are neither correct nor reliable. I feel that many employees can be paying into something that may not even exist by the time they actually need the funds. The payments being made for pension plans or social security are deducted from each employee's paycheck and are mandatory, with no choice to opt out even if employees want to. There is more information about this topic that I cover later on in the text.

CHANGES IN THE WORKPLACE

Changes in the workplace always occur and they are inevitable because of technology advancements, competition, leadership shuffles, strategy changes, economic turbulence, and market forces and so on. Changes are made at many different levels; some are minor like process changes while others are substantial like policy or leadership changes. These kinds of major changes of course impact every employee. The most drastic changes I have seen is, when a leadership shuffle occurs and new senior management appointments are made throughout the company.

This is an eye-opener since with new leadership in place, immediately new leaders have to prove their existence, start making drastic changes, appointing VPs to other sectors of the company and those VPs appoint new managers and so on down the hierarchy. Most importantly, the changes in an organization like leadership, usually introduces a different culture and environment. With changes like this, employees have no control or choice in these matters other than to wait and see what the outcome is.

So this means that if you were fitting in before enjoying your job, you may soon find out you do not fit in the new culture and environment anymore. This in fact is the uncomfortable part of this type of change since; the employee may become frustrated with the changes, because they may have lost their existing position, or have been relieved of their management duties to now have to report to a new manager. Now the demeanor of the newly assigned manager leading the department may immediately provoke employees to seek transfers to other departments within the company just for their own sanity, or if possible attempt to work for their old manager if they are still employed.

This situation presents a huge disruption and risk for an employee that has set their sights on long-term security, comfort and pension. Furthermore, maybe management will phase out the employees job and others, downsize the union workforce, so the employee may eventually not even have a job after giving the company many years of service already.

Changes can have the potential to abruptly upset the apple cart in the workplace and most importantly, current long term employees have to change their attitude and views in order to cope with new management or the company changes. If the employees don't change, they may be left with being unhappy, eventually losing morale and leaving the workplace, resulting in giving up pension, seniority and years of service. I feel that this is definitely a disadvantage.

GOING SOLO

Another employee disadvantage I found was not having the ability to go solo by starting a business. Being employed by a company the employee is obligated to perform services and tasks that are all based on their qualifications and background. With that in mind, an employee must work for the company exclusively and cannot hire other employees to increase their own salary or pay. However, even if the employee decides to open a business like a sole proprietorship on the side, this may pose as a conflict of interest with the employer, which is a breach of the employment or union agreements.

With a conflict of interest, the employee could possibly lose their job or immediately be forced to close their little company. If the employee opens a sole proprietorship successfully to make some extra money, to launch themselves into doing something new and stimulating, or to eventually be able to quit their current job may not be possible. Why? It all sounds great in theory but most of the time it doesn't really bare any fruit.

I say this because I've tried this several times myself. I found that I was lacking resources, time, and money since there was too much of an obligation to fulfil my primary function that was the main source of income I was living on. So, after plugging away, I very rarely found the time and energy to make a lift off with my own company. Then again, keep in mind the powers at hand like the CRA, HMRC, or IRS only give you so much time with a business to make a profit but only showing company losses. The company losses are usually start-up expenses you have accumulated for your small business venture.

Of course, I'm not telling you not to embark on a sole proprietorship adventure. Just because I couldn't seem to get one off the ground doesn't mean that you can't. In fact, it may end up being the most successful venture in your entire life. With that in mind, you will have to take a leap, join the contractor-corporations and may have to leave the security of being an employee.

I just want everyone to be prosperous and successful at any venture. However, most are too scared to, don't have the time, resources, and may risk their current job in the process. Besides, in order to get a business off the ground requires more time that an employee has available which poses as another disadvantage.

DEFINED HOLIDAYS

When it comes to employee holidays things are great, you go on holidays and you get paid the whole time you are gone. The disadvantage I have found is holidays are dictated by the company and their policies. Some of the common policies assign the length of allowable holidays based on employee years of service. Holiday time is commonly incremented at intervals of 5, 10 and 20 years of service. This allowable time off is also governed by labor standards or law. So, when companies are developing a policy for employee holidays they must at minimum meet or exceed labor standards for federal, provincial, or state regions.

Examples of some typical holiday periods in North America are:

- 1 to 5 years of service provides 2 or 3 weeks

- 5 to 10 years of service provides 3 to 4 weeks

- 15 years of service provides 4 to 5 weeks

- 20 years of service provides 5 to 6 weeks

When taking into account each company's policies, holiday lengths will be different, based on, the country, state, province or region you reside in. These holiday periods, are decided by law and by the union or non-union company you work for and not the employee.

Another point about holidays is in respect to union and non-union companies. In a non-unionized company, the employees must submit their proposed holiday time to their supervisor or manager, so the manager can decide whether or not the employees can take their holidays in that time period. This decision is based on, the holiday fitting into the overall work schedule or if there is a conflict. Work always takes precedence over holidays.

Unionized companies use a timetable for allotting holiday days. However, the employees choose holiday periods in a chronological order based on years of service or levels of seniority. This is another disadvantage to take into account. For instance, when working within a unionized company, the employee with the most seniority has first choice of when and how many of their holidays they will use and so on. This process continues down the seniority list until the last level of seniority personnel is reached. Usually at this point there is no ideal time period left. So, if you are at the low end of the seniority list forget that wonderful camping trip you had planned in July since it probably won't be available. Instead you will be freezing your ass off camping in November or December.

I remember this union seniority cluster very well. I was at the bottom of the seniority list and when I finally got to pick my holidays, and the only choice I had was November. Yes, in November I was freezing my ass off camping.

PIGEON HOLED

Being pigeon holed is a huge disadvantage since any employee can be pigeon holed and be held in their current position. The employee may be doing their professional best with high efficiency and productivity in order to progress into another position only later to be disappointed. The reason is, the employee does an excellent job at their current position and their collective performance is exactly what helps that team and department do a great job.

For instance, if the manager allows the employee to take-on a different position, they may not be able to find a trustworthy replacement that will do the same level of job the previous employee was doing. In other words, the employee is not going anywhere because of their great performance.

Another reason for this pigeon holing could be a silent bias against the employee that management may have, thus denying the employee to climb the company ladder to new heights while others are allowed to advance. To add to this bias, I have found that several companies only remember employee mistakes or errors and disregard any of the positive contributions and successes the employee has made.

These negative actions taken by the company directly affect the employee's morale, loyalty, belief, enthusiasm and hope. In fact, the employees have placed themselves in a dead end career without even knowing it. Unfortunately this forces the employee to seek an opportunity elsewhere even though they were true long-term employees. Do you remember what the result of changing jobs too many times is?

EXPENSE ACCOUNTS

Another item I found was the use of an expense account and having to, in most circumstances, put up my own money to cover the company as far as expenses were concerned. Using my own credit card was okay for small purchases but when purchasing items with my own credit card; management would review the purchases then remove or not cover certain purchases based on the company's disapproval or even their own biased disapproval.

In other words, I would use my own money to purchase items that were required for doing the field work, but the company wouldn't reimburse the purchase. So I was unhappy with using my credit card when having purchases scrutinized and the manager deciding what the company pays and doesn't pay. At times, I was left holding hundreds of dollars of unpaid credit card balance because the purchases were not allowed.

On other occasions, I received a corporate credit card. While using the corporate credit card, it was restricted to only cover certain items while, the need for other items couldn't be purchased. When covering the company with my own credit card or cash, the company accounting process would take long to reimburse that would incur interest rate charges on my credit card. Of course I would have to tally up the interest for payment then resubmit.

This whole process was quite frustrating. Even when using the corporate credit card, the items purchased would be scrutinized and I would owe the company for items I purchased for work, because they were not covered. So, regardless of my personal or corporate credit card, I was always getting hit with "out of pocket" expenses. I got to a point of asking for an itemized list of things that were allowed because it was too subjective.

For instance, when travelling to international work locations some field based circumstances, would max out my credit card at $50,000. I would carry the balance until the company paid the credit card. In this kind of situation the risk was very high because if the company became financially unstable or insolvent, they would leave me with the credit card bill of $50,000 to pay. I truly felt uncomfortable with carrying such large balances and debt risk especially on my own credit card.

You may be sitting there thinking that there is no risk because the company has to pay my credit card bill. Sure, but keep in mind when you are working for a company, and they become insolvent or go into receivership or bankruptcy, you won't know it until it's too late. In bankruptcy or insolvency, the money that the company has, first will go to all main credit holders.

The legal entity in charge of the bankruptcy litigation will go through the list of creditors paying each one, starting from the top which is usually banks. After they finally reach you at the very bottom of the list, they tell you there is nothing left. Consequently, you are stuck paying a company credit card bill personally. Sounds like a wonderful situation to be a part of, don't you think?

Now that we have covered what I feel are employee disadvantages, there are a few things that employees should know about, like, some of the false hopes and beliefs that employees generally have, which are controlling employee's lives every day.

Page Left Blank

THE SECRETS

In this section we look at some of the secret truths behind what some employees believe about such topics as, job security, blame, false security, climbing a corporate ladder, employee benefits packages, and pensions.

Hopefully, this will shed some insight and awareness about these topics to help open up a different perspective to think about. In fact, many employees hold these false beliefs close to heart that influence their lives and decisions.

MISSION STATEMENTS

Mission statements are written by employees and senior executive management that are about the organization or company. The mission statement defines why the company or organization exists, who their main customers or clients are, and what the company wants to achieve. Ideally, a mission statement provides the company and organization with direction, ensures decision making is in alignment to stay on course; and provides a clear purpose so business strategies can be focused on achieving the company's business goals.

However, the drawbacks to mission statements are usually unreachable, and cannot be fulfilled by the company and the organization. Additionally, if the mission statement is unreasonable, then the company may make skewed decisions based on reaching the unsound mission goal which in fact is unfavorable and damaging to the company and its future.

To further support this notion of mission statements, they are printed on fancy paper then placed in high quality frames and displayed on the walls around the company. This display of the statement is to demonstrate to employees that the organization supports goals and to remind them of this.

However, in over thirty years of being employed, I have yet to find one company that actually can stand behind their mission statement or attain it. I say this since it's all a load of hoo-ha and their actions tell the truth. I have found that many mission statements are only words with no real substance or truth.

POLICIES AND PROCEDURES

Policies and procedures of a company are created to document any company actions, activities and choices. These are all carried out within the set boundaries and limits the organization has designed. All policies and procedures impact all employees of the organization.

Company policies are written to indoctrinate their rules, beliefs, boundaries, standards and guidelines in order to reach their long term objectives. These policies are published and available to all employees. Furthermore,

HR training sessions are provided for all employees in regard to the organization's policies and ethics.

Company procedures are developed to support the organization's policies. Procedures capture step-by-step methods in order to create repeatable practices within the company that are used during daily operations. Employees are trained to instill awareness and teach procedural practices used by the organization.

Again, in over thirty years of employment, I have yet to find one company that actually conforms to their own policies, and procedures. Most polices are just words with no corresponding action deeming them as worthless. In truth, I found many of the company policies and even some standards and procedures are sadly enough, overridden by management's egotism, favoritism and power.

THE BLAME GAME

Another popular false truth that I have found amongst employees is blaming the company or their employer. The employee's attitudes and beliefs make them blame the employer for their own personal financial situation. The blame stems from the employee holding a certain position in the company and receiving a corresponding salary. However, as time passes they start to accumulate debt, make purchases and establish a certain level of lifestyle. Unknown to the employee is that they are living beyond their means or affordability. The spending for an elevated lifestyle continues until, the true financial situation comes to the forefront.

The reality strikes the employee and starts to feel that money is becoming scarcer. This means that shortly after being paid, the employee has less and less cash in their pocket. This is considered as a financial warning sign or pinch that the employee usually ignores. Nonetheless, the employee continues with spending and other habits with no change. About six months after the initial pinch, suddenly everything all at once seems to come to a screeching halt. This is what I call the financial squeeze and the current financial reality coming to the forefront. This is when the employee starts to feel the real pain related to the financial conditions brought on by the employee's own desire to live a better life style. This is in fact when the employee has no cash except to look at bills and make decisions to choose which bill to skip, in order to maintain cash in hand and spending.

The employee at this point begins to ask questions about the situation like, why don't I have any money? Why did this happen? Is my rent too high? Did my car insurance increase? Where is all my money going? The answers are quite simple, since it is the employee that has exclusively created the financial mess. Their answer to the situation is that they are not being paid enough. With this deduction, the employee goes to the boss to ask for a raise. The result is the employee finds out they are being paid the maximum amount for their current position. The refusal of having a raise makes the employee frustrated and upset. Since now the financial pressures and pain, as well as, the rejection of getting a raise, together change the attitude of the employee. To protect their own feelings and dignity they start to blame the company or the employer for not paying enough and start looking for another job.

The reality with these kinds of situations is this: The employer has a number of positions within the company that all have corresponding salary ranges. Each salary range is calculated to ensure it is cost effective and aligned with salary benchmarks for the specific industry. This allows the company to not only be competitive with paying salaries to their employees but also enables the company to remain being profitable and a competitive business. In other words, there are salary limitations for any position in any company even though employees don't understand this nor want to.

They in turn would rather blame the company instead, of facing the errors they have made with their own finances. The employee feels it's the company's fault that they have financial problems which is false. There is only so much money an employee can get paid regardless of their occupation whether they are a, technician, auto mechanic, document manager, doctor, accountant, senior manager, plumber, carpenter, cost engineer, design engineer, welder, senior manager, CEO, VP, admin support, IT professional, and so on. There is always a hierarchy for positions, pay scale and the return on investment of each position. *This means that pay is calculated based on how much financial impact the position has on the company.*

For instance, a manager gets paid more than their subordinates because of their skill sets, training, responsibilities, education, experience, competencies and the overall impact the position has within the company. Another angle is a company's research and development (R &D) department and employees are like a money pit. The R&D requires large amounts of resources and money without directly providing an actual return on the investment. However this group is essential for the company's innovations, competitive edge and future, which in the end provides an intangible return on investment. In fact, without the R&D department the company's future would be short lived.

So the employee blaming the company is not realistic. The truth lies in self-reflection to see what the problem is and what is causing their financial problems. Also, if they want to increase their salary to elevate their lifestyle and quality of life, they must first increase their education, training, skill sets, experience, and competencies.

CAREER ADVANCEMENT

Many employees believe they have the ability and a clear pathway to climb the corporate ladder, and to get a better paying position. Employees think that there is opportunity for everyone and that any employee can climb the ladder if they choose to. This may be true but the reality is that some management will use favoritism, bias, grudges and power to bypass them from advancing. In other words not all employees are eligible for career advancements even though they may qualify more so than others. Another downside of career advancement is when employees are self-centered, power hungry and egotistical. They are only geared and driven to advance themselves and don't care what they have to do to get there. People with this kind of attitude, only introduce egotism, back stabbing, favoritism, humiliation, discrimination, and other related negative behaviors into the workplace. This is all for their personal power and gain, with no regard, for anyone else.

Of course, these types of behaviors only make the workplace an undesirable and unpleasant place to work because many people get hurt on both professional and personal levels. These go-getter cut throats that have no conscience, really don't give two shits about co-workers, their wellbeing only themselves. When egotistical types like this make it to management, they, because of the abrasive demeanor, immediately lose many of their subordinates who are in fact excellent employees.

Throughout my twenties and part of my thirties I was driven as well but, never pissed people off, stepped on their toes, wasn't a cutthroat, or a bully. For instance, when I started at my first real career industry job, I worked long hours and studied hard to learn about the equipment I was working with. This was all so I could achieve and move from a trainee position to a junior level position. I achieved the junior level within 7 months while the average timeframe was 12 to 18 months.

Furthermore, I was able to show and convince upper management of my abilities and knowledge. This allowed me to enter the bidding for a Middle East technical advisor position only after 2 ½ years of employment. Usually the bidding process consisted of senior employees which have 7 to 10 years of experience. In fact senior candidates could take any opportunity they wanted to, reducing my chances to almost zero except for this one. Many candidates hesitated to apply because the position was in an unstable and precarious region of the world.

This position was located in Ahwaz, Iran, a highly volatile place just six months after the eight year Iran–Iraq war was halted. There was no peace or war declared and everything was in limbo. In fact, there were over 500,000 Iraqi soldiers still lined up along the border. I was afraid, but it didn't deter me because I was determined and driven to become a specialist, a technical advisor in the Middle East.

I played the odds anyway, and was the first candidate to apply for the position. I acted on the premise of probability, meaning other people's fears being greater than my own. I also found that most of the senior candidates were married with children and speculated that they wouldn't take a risk. While I on the other hand, felt that I was a prime candidate being single, with no ties and ready to go. Based on all of my assumptions, I knew this would be my only chance to work in an international location.

In the end my assumptions were correct, I won the bidding since no one else wanted to go but one other person who became my shift relief. Besides being a technical advisor, I wanted to see and experience another country being adventurous in my mid-twenties and I never stepped foot into a foreign country before. Consequently, after winning the bid, my first country travelled was going to be Iran or how the locals would call it *"Eron."*

Before embarking on the journey, I didn't research Iran like others on the crew; I on the other hand was more interested in speaking to the Iranians directly. All I remember throughout my childhood adolescents was that Iran and Iraq did this and that, and was unstable. I didn't ever really understand what the whole fight was between Iran and Iraq. It was absolutely something that I could never imagine until I arrived there.

Upon arrival, I realized the work location was situated in a war zone only 40 miles from the Iraqi border. In fact the Iraqis came within 3 miles from Ahwaz. This city became a safe haven for migrant refugees that came from the war torn surrounding communities and a main border city, called Abadan. According to the locals, Abadan had universities and was a thriving city that unfortunately was destroyed and didn't exist anymore.

Now, Ahwaz was a city of over 2 million people, with electrical power continuously load shedding, buildings blown apart into rubble, many injured, and with countless people mourning for their lost loved ones. Shockingly many people I spoke to had lost 8 to 10 family members during the war. It was truly unfortunate, painful and heartbreaking for those innocent families and people. To me it was horrifying, disturbing, and laborious. I could not relate to this harsh reality especially coming from North America where there is no war and people are driven by money and excelling at their careers.

During my twenties to my mid-thirties I had the drive to succeed, excel and get to the top, climb a mountain, and of course, had that invincible, "I'll be president one day" kind of attitude. After so many years of succeeding at climbing the ladders and taking on roles of field supervisor, technical manager, training manager, technical advisor, and project manager, I realized that all this hype about management positions in my opinion… wasn't worth it.

In management or supervisory roles, you are expected to take full responsibility, put in extra hours and effort to do whatever it takes. If you recall my technical manager story, all of the worries, stress, anxiety and extra time were shortening my lifespan, and in the end it was never really worth the extra money. All of these things only add pressure and stress that weakens our immune system and induces physical illness, such as irritable bowel, high blood pressure, acid reflux, ulcers, nervous conditions, and creates insomnia. Then we have to find ways to cope with these conditions of anxiety, tensions and worries.

To cope with the added pressures and stress some people turn to smoking, drinking and drugs, while others use exercise and a fitness routine. Many people also resort to their physician prescribing medications for depression, anxiety and panic such as, Prozac, Paxil, Zoloft or other serotonin-reuptake-inhibitor medications (SSRIs). So, is management for you or worth it?

What I found was that the higher and higher you climb the ladder the responsibilities and stress increase proportionally. In truth this all added up to months and years of my personal time gone. This was time I had lost that I will never get back, ever. Sorry, but after all of the management experiences I've had; I'd rather make a couple of bucks less per hour and go home at 5 pm every night, so I can relax, and enjoy my personal time. As far as I am concerned, let others worry about it and have the stress for the extra bucks because…life is just too short.

JOB GUARANTEES

As far as job security goes, having a job without ever losing it… well it doesn't exist, because anyone can lose their job at the drop of a hat regardless; whether you are a laborer, supervisor, senior manager, VP, director or even

CEO. Generally, in some circumstances job loss can happen quickly, while in other situations it is tardy. Most importantly it "can" happen; and I have seen and experienced it.

As any employee, even if you are fired or let go, there is at most times, a severance package, and employment insurance benefits to fall back on. Even if there isn't a package, it may cost the company 20, or 30 or even 50 grand but who cares, you are still out of a job. Then, you have to pay tax on the money they give you, and if it's a wrongful dismissal you also pay your lawyer to win a lawsuit.

If we also add in economic or market forces, such as, commodity market free fall just like oil in the past couple of years has fallen from $150 per barrel to below $30. This itself creates havoc on the job front as well as impacting any commodity based economies like, Saudi, Qatar, Kuwait, USA, Canada, Norway, UK and many others causing slow growth and high unemployment. This only proves that, no one or any company is immune to deep economic impact since it affects all industries anywhere in the world.

However, some employees are oblivious to market impacts, believing nothing will happen and place their trust in their employer. They believe that the company will continue to prosper regardless of the economic conditions. Of course many companies do weather such storms and survive the economic turmoil but do not remain unscathed. Keep in mind that the largest cost and expense for a company is always the employee payroll.

For example, just recently, Hewlett Packard announced that it was cutting 30,000 employees. If we do a quick calculation and crunch some numbers, it gives us a clearer picture of why their decision was to let go 30,000 employees. Generally, if each employee's average salary was $36,000 a year or $3000 a month that would equate to a savings of $90 million per month or $1.08 billion a year not including the cost of the employee benefits packages. With benefit packages this would add an additional 30 percent or $27 million a month or $324 million a year.

Another item to add stems from employees thinking they have a guaranteed job, especially those in unions, which is never the case. Many employees believe they will never get fired or laid-off and nothing will ever change. The employees also believe that even if the economy faces huge commodity downturns like in the oil industry they will be untouched. Guess again. For example, the oil sands, in Canada, alone were hit very hard and job losses were happening by the tens of thousands, including those in unions. Moreover, in the US, the situation wasn't much different. In Canada the total job loss so far according to an August 31, 2015, CBC article is 35,000 to date.

This article is found at the following URL:

http://www.cbc.ca/news/business/alberta-has-lost-35-000-oilpatch-jobs-petroleum-producers-say-1.3208717

According to the April 14, 2015, Wall Street Journal article, over 100,000 oil workers worldwide have lost their jobs, so far. The full article can be found at the following URL:

http://www.wsj.com/articles/oil-layoffs-hit-100-000-and-counting-1429055740

The whole belief about being guaranteed has no bearing or truth since all of us on the whole, have no guarantee in anything in our lives. Moreover, especially what a company decides. Companies are doing whatever is necessary to please shareholders, to endure economic forces, like layoffs, and program cuts, and some companies will even merge in order to survive.

Throughout my experiences, I have seen many situations of high unemployment when people lose their jobs, such as, directors, VPs, CEOs, laborers, engineers, sales people, and others. I have taken a reduction in pay, taken time off with no pay, to accommodate my employer. I have also outright lost jobs, because of economic or commodity market downturns.

In reality, there is no such thing as job security since to have full and complete security, would mean that there would be no risk. In truth though, risk can only be reduced and minimized, not eliminated. Therefore, risks always exist and with it job security risks. However, in order to improve your chances of having more job security than others is to be flexible even if it means taking pay cuts, time off and other measures the company feels are necessary.

FALSE SENSE OF SECURITY

Some privately owned companies are still doing business by pushing paper unlike the big kids on the block that have elaborate and innovative systems. Not all companies are at a high tech stage nor do they want to be. The reason is, there is no need because, things seem to be running smoothly, they are still in business, making a profit and the employees have been working there forever.

With that in mind, the company has employees that have been there for over 20 to 30 years or more and know everything to do with the company and their processes. Within these companies there has never been a real need for formal documentation only a few informal documents that are used. Therefore, there have never been any recorded or documented policies, processes, manuals, work instructions, procedures, and guidelines to support the company or new or existing employees. Instead the company relies on the long term senior employee's knowledge, experience and subjectivity.

These senior employees are considered by many as old school. These individuals believe that the knowledge they carry in their head, is their job security, meaning that they will never get fired or let go. This in reality is a false sense of security especially with today's technologies, and educated workforce. Anyone can be replaced at any time, regardless of their extensive experience, knowledge or position they retain. When employees believe that retaining information will prevent them from being fired, laid-off or replaced, it is in truth, all false.

Even if the company lost the individuals who retain all the knowledge, other people can replace those people, which may cause only temporary delays and setbacks for the company. However, the company moves forward regardless of who quits, dies, or leaves. Companies have established a customer base over their lifetime of business that has generated millions of dollars of income, each and every year and that continues on year after year.

A company's whole function, or products, services or whatever they do, does not all stand because of one person or a couple of people. For instance, the owner and founder of Microsoft had some visionary gifts, yet, there are always others who exist in the world or even within the company that have similar or even superior vision.

Consequently, every company does require leadership. However, the company is in business because of all of the company employees combined carrying out each function and all of the tasks to implement the leadership ideas. Together, this is what makes the company successful and what they are today and beyond.

PENSION MY ASS

The Magical Day

I discussed pensions in an earlier section however this section covers a few different viewpoints about pension. While working for many companies, especially unionized ones, I discovered many employees were focused on retirement. They were waiting to reach a magical age of 65, and were just counting the days until they retire.

Meanwhile, these same employees dread getting up every morning, day after day, year after year and going into a workplace they despise. Most importantly, they are unaware that as they continue towards retirement they are actually working themselves into the grave due to the stress. To support this view, according to the October 10th, 2013 Forbes article called, "Unhappy Employees Outnumber Happy Ones by Two to One Worldwide" which states that; "there are twice as many workers that hate their job than those who love their job." In fact, many people would leave their job in a second if they had the courage and confidence or the money. Consequently, many are stuck in the same rut until retirement regardless of their true wishes.

I also learned that many employees' main focus was to wait for retirement; these employees sit at home, save their money, and refrain from pursuing things they like to do and enjoy. Their main excuse for denying themselves was they could do these things at retirement. Some of the things they would put on hold were travel, painting, writing, art, gardening, singing, playing piano, second language, dancing and other activities. Consequently, these employees place their lives on hold until their magical retirement age of sixty five and then they start living.

Many people don't realize that as we continue to age, we change mentally and physically throughout the aging cycle. Our biological changes all affect our skin, bones, joints, muscles, body shape, our looks, teeth and gums, hair and nails, immune system, memory, hearing, vision, smell and taste, bowel and bladder function, as well as, sleep patterns. Hey is there anything that I left out? Seriously, these things change regardless of our inadequate diets or our vices.

Even with all these age related changes occurring many of us keep doing the same things as we did in our youth. With that in mind, many individuals health starts to deteriorate because of their, continued use of alcohol, cigarettes, drugs, illegal or OTC. For instance, according to the world health organization (WHO) over 80% of the world's 1 billion smokers live in low to middle income countries. Tobacco at minimum kills at least 50% of its users.

To add to this most of us have an unhealthy diet and poor eating habits. Many of us are unaware of our metabolic changes which make us gain weight very rapidly that may lead to obesity and diabetes. This change usually begins in our forties and weight gain is so quick, in fact, just by looking at a box of cookies you can immediately feel your ass grow! On top of it all, many of us also don't exercise which is a main ingredient to combat the effects of aging.

So, if you add all of this up it's a perfect formula for serious health problems in our later years. According to some surveys those with poor health before retirement generally only live about 18 months after retirement. It has also been found that early retirement at 55 compared to 65 equates to earlier death too.

Putting life on hold and waiting until retirement, isn't reasonable at all. I stress this since; as we get older many of us are not as energetic, mobile, flexible, and agile, as we were during our youthful years. Even though we still can maintain physical fitness and retain muscle mass just like we had in our thirties. Waiting a long time for something in life isn't living, since with life, we just never know what lies ahead like, serious illness, accidents, arthritis, heart problems, stroke, hip replacement, vision impairment or loss, heart attack, high blood pressure, glaucoma, diabetes, obesity, or other diseases and even sudden death.

So living today, at least allows us to live each day, to do things we like and enjoy without depriving ourselves which doesn't require retirement. We can do it today, retired or not and live that passion out while we still have our youth, mobility and health. There is nothing in this world to stop you from learning pottery, dancing, painting, art, writing, piano, gardening and so on... except you.

When we live in the "now", we are living day by day, enjoying each day as they pass. Waiting for something of course can have exceptions. For example, when I was working at this company, I remember being in a conversation with a couple of co-workers. We got on the topic of lotteries. One of the workers immediately piped up and said, "If I won the lottery, I would go shit right on top of the director's desk!" and then I asked, "Why wait until you win the lottery?"

For quite a while now over two decades, I have lost confidence in predicting the future and stopped living in fear and anxiety worried about retirement and the magical day in my life. I decided to join, not the freedom 55 plan but the freedom 90 plan instead.

Pension Ya Right

Many people are employees mainly because of the bright light at the end of the tunnel called pension. In many people's minds, government or company based pensions or even their own pension savings are full proof because these funds will be there when employees retire. For the fortunate ones, yes there will be a pension plan or a retirement savings account with funds. However, many people still ask which kind of plan is the better one to have.

The most popular company pension plans involve two types which are a "defined benefit" and a "defined contribution" pension scheme. A defined benefit pension plan is when the company guarantees a pension income for each employee at the end of their service. The amount of the pension payment is derived by using a set of metrics. These metrics are based on, the years of being a member of the plan, the employee's income average in the last 5 years of service including overtime and what the employee's average earnings were during the whole period of service. Using the metrics and having a set retirement date, the company pension fund will guarantee the employee a pension income amount based on the pension metric calculations.

In my humble opinion, a defined benefit plan is the best one to have. However, the failure of many pension plans is starting to rise as well as, the reduction of pension payment amounts. Many companies year after year, default on retirement payments to employees due to the pension fund falling short financially or complete failure, thus becoming non-existent. Some of the reasons for shortfalls may be attributed to,

- Senior management redirects pension fund capital to be used in other projects or as venture capital with no payback

- Companies managing and investing the retirement funds make poor investment decisions

- The company does not calculate and forecast the funds requirements correctly. Leaving too little money to accommodate the current or future retirees, thus forced to cut payments

- Unforeseen market and economic forces and instabilities creating massive or even systemic pension fund losses or failure, or

- The company itself fails

The disturbing outcome of these shortfalls is only to abruptly leave their loyal employees with no pension income or to drastically reduce their current or future pension income. On top of it all many retirees have very little savings, which is totally devastating especially in their later years. In truth, these retirees have been loyal to the same company for 20 to 40 years of their prime working life only to end up, broke with no pension and with a broken promise.

As an employee with a defined benefit fund it's up to you to do some research to find out the financial state of your pension fund. In the US, you can do this by requesting the information such as a summary annual report, and look at the return or performance of the fund. You can also look at the minimum funding standards section of the report which states if the fund actually meets such standards. In addition, you can also search the Pension Benefits Guaranty Corporation (PBGC) which is a government agency that insures private pensions in the US. They can be accessed online at www.pbgc.gov

In Canada, there are no guarantees of private pension plans. Only one in the province of Ontario called Pension Benefits Guarantee Fund which guarantees up to $1,000 a month under certain circumstances, whatever that means? Also according to a study by the Dominion Bond Rating Service or DBRS, which states, of 461 plans in Canada, the U.S., Japan and Europe, found the average funding level of pension funds in 2012 had fallen to only 78%. DBRS considers funding levels under 80% to represent a "danger zone." For more information visit the DBRS site at www.dbrs.com.

I have seen defined benefit pension funds fade quickly from the pension world. Many companies are dropping the defined benefit scheme to move to defined contribution. The reason is pensioners are living longer and interest rate returns are very, very low resulting in these pension schemes having inadequate funds available for all of their dedicated hard working employees. This strongly suggests the defined pension will become a thing of the past because of the lack of funds and the company also carries all of the defined benefit plan risks.

Now companies are basically handing over the liability and risk by switching to a defined contribution type plan. This means that it is up to the employee to make decisions based on what shares, mutual funds or other investment instruments will be used for investing for the future of their own pension fund. With a defined contribution plan, employees contribute to their own pension fund and in turn the company contributes by matching the employee's contribution to a maximum yearly amount.

This contribution by the company and the pension vehicle itself is still a good plan, because the employee has more control. However, this also means the employee carries all of the risk and liability. In other words, if poor investment decisions are made by the employee it could result in substantial or catastrophic losses, which may result in the employee's fund having a small amount of money or none at all.

For instance, if an employee decided to buy and invest in tech stock ABC company shares at $110 each then....to find out a few years later that the shares are now only worth $1.50 each. The employee would have full responsibility with the decision to buy the shares in the first place and to cope with the huge loss of over 98% of their pension fund. Keep in mind with this schema, there is no blaming the company, because it is the employee's decision, not the company's.

I use this simple scenario as an example, because most people just make a decision and leave it. They follow ostrich methods of investing by sticking their head in the sand. Employees think and believe that it'll take care of itself. This means the employees don't watch it, and check on it on a regular basis. They at some point in the future will decide to look at their fund to realize they have been slaughtered in the stock market and by then it's too late.

This type of pension scheme is also a disadvantage for many people. The reason is many employees have no real experience with investments and many trust investment representatives at banks and other institutions. They believe these representatives will protect their money and provide instrumental investment advice.

The truth is, investment representatives do not manage a person's money, nor do they have sound knowledge of where to place your retirement money or savings. They in fact only follow company policies and software to set up a portfolio for their client. The software chooses what sectors to invest their client's money according to their client's age and risk threshold.

Many other investment gurus suggest that you have a balanced portfolio. So when you are losing your shirt in one sector, the others, should be increasing in value balancing everything out. I strongly disagree with this because many sectors can free fall simultaneously thus creating a high potential of deep losses. A simple suggestion is that a money market fund is the most stable that doesn't offer much growth but it allows you to retain your money with little loss, if any, regardless of economic turmoil or market downturns.

Each and every time there is a market crash or meltdown, like in 1929, 1971, 1987, 1989, 1990, 2000, 2007, 2008 and 2010 people and companies have lost billions or even trillions. Most of these losses are stock market based investments resulting in wiping out retirement funds belonging to companies, governments, people and even pensioners! Regardless, losses can occur within, government pension funds, defined contribution, defined benefit, and personal pension savings accounts because many are positioned in high risk investments.

So, there is always a very strong possibility of default of defined benefits and defined contribution pension funds because almost all rely on stock market based investing for getting returns. During market meltdowns, like any in history results in, many people are left, time after time, with minimal amounts of cash in pension funds, with no savings, only to start over trying to find a job to make ends meet at retirement age.

For example, I recall during the 1999-2000 downturns where all the high-technology companies were way overvalued, one like a communications company called Nortel. Pensions were buying blocks of Nortel shares at their peak of $124 a share in August 2000. Then to quickly find out that share prices were based on hype, and the shares started to free fall to a value of $0.27. The disintegration of Nortel came to fruition in January 2009 when Nortel did not exist anymore and filed for Chapter 11. So where are all the, pension plan gurus that were managing the plans and buying these Nortel shares and others like it at their peak? Sadly enough, I can only guess that they are still employed managing some other pension plan and getting their commissions and pay.

Another point I want to mention is about government pensions that are comparable to the current defined benefits plans which are also in trouble. I include these because everyone seems to be contributing into something that is mandatory and may not receive anything just when they need it the most. So I have to ask, how does that work?

Well… it doesn't. For instance, in the US according to a Nov. 14th 2014 Forbes article called, "Bad News For State Public Pensions Plans" states that, "In 2013 state pension plans were underfunded by a staggering $4.1 trillion. In 2014 that number has risen to $4.7 trillion. Even though the economy has been improving and there is more talk about state budget surpluses than deficits, states are not addressing this major budgetary issue." The same belief about the Canada pension plan which is the Canadian governments defined benefit plan is that it won't exist when most of the current population is baby boomers that will retire within the next two decades. To learn about how the Canada Pension plan works visit the following site.

http://www.servicecanada.gc.ca/eng/services/pensions/cpp/retirement/

Also an excellent article in the Huffington Post, dated March 30, 2015, entitled, "After 50 Years of the Canada

Pension Plan We've Run Off Course", clearly states the pension situation and how the general public is set up for retirement. This quote from the article tells us a lot about the conditions:

"But the typical 35-year-old today is saving less than half of what their parents did at that age. Three-quarters of those working in the private sector don't have access to an employer-sponsored pension plan. And of those who are within 10 years of retirement, less than one-third have $100,000 or more set aside to sustain themselves. Another third have no retirement savings at all."

If you would like to read the full Huffington Post article, go to the following URL:

http://www.huffingtonpost.ca/ralph-goodale/canada-pension-plan_b_6967640.html

With the majority of Canada's population having no savings while their retirement is imminent, it strongly suggest there will be harsh consequences coming soon for many private or government employees when it comes to their magical pension fund. Additionally, the government plans to increase employee's contribution to the Canada pension plan to make up the shortfalls. To find out more about increases visit the following sites:

http://www.bnn.ca/cpp-reforms-to-provide-little-benefit-for-many-canadian-workers-report-1.525914 http://opinion.financialpost.com/2011/06/09/dont-double-down-on-a-big-cpp-cd-howe-warns/

On another front in the US, an article dated, March 17th 2015 in the LA times, clearly explains the loss of pensions, in regard to the California Public Employees' Retirement System, known as CalPERS. The article states, "As millions of private employees lost their pension benefits in recent years, government workers rested easy, believing that their promised retirements couldn't be touched."

The article continues to state that, with the demand for pension funds growing at astronomical proportions, pensions are becoming a problem for cities across the state of California. Californians owe nearly $200 billion for pensions promised to state and local government workers, according to a nonprofit think tank, California Common Sense. So is there any pension guarantees when the article states:

"San Bernardino could be the first city in California to consider cutting worker pensions in a bankruptcy."

You can find this article at the following URL:

http://www.latimes.com/business/la-fi-pension-controversy-20150317-story.html

To add some more factual data to the pension fund failure a chart from the Pension Benefit Guaranty Corporation lists the top ten pension failures. The totals according to the data for all ten companies pension fund failures are:

- Total amount of claims, $27 billion

- Vested participants, 543,875

- Average Claim per Person, $49,933

So, what happens to all of those employees who are looking forward to that magical day of retirement and are sixty five? Those who have very little built up savings, all relying on their government or company based pensions. Are they supposed to keep working and start saving in their mid-sixties? What happens to those dedicated employees who have worked all their lives and looked forward to a defined benefit pension that has failed or defaulted? Or the retirees of defined contribution pension that have been wiped out by market forces? On top of having market meltdowns and potential catastrophic losses to pension funds there is yet another problem looming with defined benefit pensions that are not indexed.

Indexing

This is another fact about pensions however this topic refers specifically to defined benefit pension plan indexing. Indexing, what does that mean? When the pension plan is indexed it means that the amount the recipient receives will increase based on the rate of inflation or the consumer price index (CPI).

The CPI is derived by the cost of a fixed basket of commodities or goods, such as food, shelter, clothing, and transportation, health care and so on. The CPI or rate of inflation is examined each year by the government or controller of the company pension fund to determine how much the pension fund distributions will increase. In other words the recipient's pension increases along with the increase in cost of living. What does it mean if the pension is not indexed?

Without indexing the plan will pay the recipient a defined amount each month. The same payment amount will continue regardless of the inflation level. Therefore, an increase in inflation, results in goods and services becoming more expensive to the consumer. This directly affects the cost of living for each person but the pension payout is the same amount. This in turn means that the pensioner can buy less and less goods as each year passes.

For example, if Hillary and Bernie who live in the United States were pensioners and retired in the year 2000, then they would be paid in "2000 dollars" not "2016 dollars". Consequently, if they purchased grocery items in 2000 for $100 with inflation those same goods in 2014 would cost them $137.48, an increase of 37.48 %. This means that they have lost 37.48% of their pension income and purchasing power because it was not indexed to account for inflation adjustments. So do your own due diligence and find out if your defined benefit pension is an indexed pension, because if it's not, in the long run, your pension income purchasing power will eventually be depleted.

So keep in mind that the longer you live, the more your purchasing power is reduced. This in fact is one of the main reasons people have very little or no savings or are broke in their later years. As prices rise retirees in turn are forced to subsidize their pension income by using their savings especially in times like today with very low interest rate returns. Inflation can deplete your pension and savings or in other words inflation ends up eating your money.

A last point to mention is about inflation effects and your defined contribution pension or any investment, for that matter. Note that inflation always plays a significant role in your investing, if you want it to or not. Because the truth is, if your defined contribution pension fund, or savings account, rate of return does not meet or exceed the current inflation rate, your money is always losing purchasing power just as a non-indexed pension fund does. The reason for this reduction in purchasing power is the "real interest rate" of the investment, which represents the actual growth rate. Consequently, many people are unaware that a, "real interest rate" exists.

For example, if your defined contribution investment is at a rate of 2% per year and the inflation rate is 1.5% the real interest rate your fund is growing at is calculated as follows:

Real Interest Rate = Current Rate of Return–Inflation Rate

Real Interest Rate = 2% – 1.5%

=0.5%

Therefore, the real growth rate or real rate of return for your defined contribution pension investment is 0.5%. Remember that inflation is always occurring in the financial system otherwise the system doesn't work.

After discussing all of these pension perspectives, are you ready as an employee to have the rug pulled out from underneath you just before you retire or while you are retired? I would say no. Sure there is a guarantee and that is *YOU*, being in charge of your retirement funds by keeping it safe, sound and continually monitoring the health of your company pension and government based pensions.

Richard Renstone

IT'S A WRAP

This wraps up *Permanent Employee: The Pros, Cons and Secrets*. Within this book we looked at and explored what it means to be an employee and the general mindset permanent employees have. We continued to discuss the advantages and disadvantages of being an employee and also exposed some of the subconscious secrets employees have believed for years; which have been controlling employee's lives by inducing fear and anxiety both on the job front and financially.

Throughout this book I shared some of my stories, personal experiences and nightmares that I have had while dealing with different companies and employment situations. This was all to jar your mindset so you can see that there are other options, beliefs, truths and attitudes about being a permanent employee.

After reading this book I hope you have a better grasp of your employee situation, your future as an employee and an understanding of pensions so you can secure your own future. By being in the know, there is no need to believe in false truths anymore and to be controlled any longer. You have to do what suits you and what you feel comfortable with because everyone is different.

Keep in mind that working is a large part of life and at times, a lot of it may be frustrating and unfair but on the other hand it can be very, rewarding, uplifting, fun and fulfilling especially when you have a positive outlook.

I can only hope this book has given you some foundational insight, a new path and to understand what it means to be an employee so you can start to live your life without false fears, be happy, and enjoy your career. I would like to thank you for letting me enter your life. Before I sign off I would like to leave you with a few thoughts.

To make substantial changes in your career you must also change your behaviors by introducing and following best practices. My book called, *Permanent Employee: Best Practices Handbook* provides you with over fifty life altering practices that will substantially change your life and career.

"You are solely responsible for what kind of work life and lifestyle you would like to have, because no one else knows only you so it's up to you no one else. So whatever you do, do it with honesty and integrity."

Thanks,

Richard Renstone

NOTE TO THE READER

If you liked *Permanent Employee: The Pros, Cons and Secrets* then check out my next book entitled, *Permanent Employee: Best Practices Handbook* which offers over fifty career changing practices that will:

- Improve your work life
- Advance your career
- Increase your pay
- Make you a key employee and much, much more!

Together these two books are the only cutting edge permanent employee book set on the market that is written from a personal point of view and over three decades of experience.

See you in the *Best Practices Handbook*!

ABOUT THE AUTHOR

Richard Renstone grew up in a small northern city in Canada, and completed an associate's degree in Electronics Engineering.

Soon after, Renstone acquired a job in the oil and gas industry, launching him into various countries in South America, Europe, Middle East, Far East and Australia during which evaded death upon two occasions.

A decade later, Renstone changed careers to become a technical publication author and instructional designer. During this time he acquired two undergraduate degrees, a Bachelor of Arts and Bachelor of Metaphysical Science. Renstone is a lifelong learner and continues to acquire specialized knowledge and certifications.

Today Renstone is a writer, author, and has published many books and will continue to write and travel the world.

If you have any comments or questions please feel free to contact me via email at richardrenstone@gmail.com or find me on Twitter @RichardRenstone

Other Books By The Author

Permanent Employee: The Pros, Cons and Secrets (2018)

Permanent Employee: Best Practices Handbook (2018)

Make Your Career Great Again! (2018)